Island Barbecue

Island Barbecue

Spirited Recipes from the Caribbean

by Dunstan
A. Harris

Illustrations by
Brooke Scudder

CHRONICLE BOOKS · SAN FRANCISCO

Library of Congress Cataloging-in-Publication Data.

Harris, Dunstan A., 1947
    Island barbecue : spirited recipes from the Carribbean /
by Dunstan Harris : illustrations by Brooke Scudder.
      p. cm.
    Includes bibliographical references and index.
    ISBN 0-8118-0510-7
    1. Barbecue cookery--Caribbean Area. 2. Cookery, Caribbean.
    I Title
    TX840.B3H377 1995
    641.5784--dc20   94-13262
                                 CIP

Printed in Hong Kong.

Distributed in Canada by Raincoast Books,
8680 Cambie Street, Vancouver, B.C. V6P 6M9

10 9 8 7 6 5 4 3

Chronicle Books
275 Fifth Street
San Francisco, CA 94103

Contents

Dedication

To the memory of my dear, departed mother, Doris Johnston. It was her wonderful culinary innovations that whetted my appetite and her recipes via long-distance phone calls that gave me true direction.

Acknowledgments

Every cookbook author needs that special literary agent who believes in his or her next project. Without **Richard Derus of the Claudia Menza Literary Agency, and Ms. Menza herself,** *Island Barbecue* would still be in mothballs. Their faith and persistence are greatly responsible for the publication of this book.

To my publisher, Chronicle Books, I am truly grateful for their faith that island cuisine has a place in the American melting pot.

To my wife, Helen, and children, Jamal and Alisha, who have always shown remarkable understanding and patience when I've neglected them for the typewriter and test kitchen—thank you.

Many thanks to Marion Sherman, the producer of a possible TV cooking show that I will host. She inundated me with books and articles on barbecuing.

To Walter Richards for some excellent research material, and *George Marcelle* for his insights on island barbecue and his assistance with some recipes.

Finally, a special thanks to Jo-Ann Spence, my word processor. Her speed in returning corrected and completed copy was phenomenal.

Preface  **half-century ago**, in many Caribbean islands, food was cooked outdoors year-round—a necessity rather than a celebration. In her book, *Tell My Horse: Voodoo and Life in Haiti and Jamaica*, celebrated American author and anthropologist Zora Neale Hurston observed in 1936 while visiting a group in a Jamaican Maroon village, ". . . there was no stove in all Accompong. The cooking, ironing, and whatever else is done, is done over an open fire." Although in today's modern island society that observation no longer applies, back then it was fact.

Island Barbecue looks at barbecue in the Caribbean from the time Columbus arrived there to find the Amerindians cooking meat and fish on green wood racks over an open fire—*boucan*—and renamed it *barbacoa*, or barbecue. Coupled with the Amerindians' grilling prowess was their use of the chile pepper *capsicum annum*, known as habañeros in the southwestern United States or Scotch Bonnets in much of the English-speaking Caribbean. Chiles were eaten in every conceivable manner by the Amerindians. As Bernardino de Sahagun, a Spanish observer and chronicler, wrote in 1569, they ate " . . . frog with green chiles, newt with yellow chiles, tadpoles with small chiles, and lobster with red chiles." Many of the recipes reflect this spicy tradition—a hallmark of Caribbean cuisine.

Every backyard cook owes the Amerindians a debt of gratitude, for it is their legacy that we so ardently pursue every time we light up the grill. In the United States, barbecuing has a festive tradition. Barbecuing was an integral part of cooking in the Old South, where many plantations had their own master barbecuer, also known as a pitmaster. He did everything from tending the fire to basting the meat just right. He was also responsible for creating his own sauce, which was crucial to the success of the barbecue. The pitmaster could attain great importance, and, often, he and his owner would profit greatly by selling his services to other plantations.

Americans are always eager to try new dishes, and many now enjoy Caribbean food. With the proliferation of three- and four-star restaurants offering Caribbean dishes, and the success of a recent slew of cookbooks, island cuisine is experiencing a meteoric climb in popularity. This new craving can perhaps be attributed to the increase of tourists to Caribbean ports. On their return home, the newly initiated seek out tropical cuisine, perhaps to evoke pleasant beachside memories.

While on catering jobs, attending food shows, or doing cooking demonstrations and cookbook signings, I inevitably field questions about Jamaican jerk cooking. The word *jerk* has legitimate roots. "Jirk," the Old English translation for the Spanish *charqui*, described the Amerindian method of preserving beef (today's beef jerky), which in pre-Columbian times was sun dried. This method is attributed to the Quechua Indians of Peru, but the method migrated northwards to the Caribbean, Jamaica in particular, with their cousins the Arawaks, and underwent some culinary changes. In current usage, jerk, which also underwent a spelling change, refers to the seasoning and cooking of meats, seafood, and vegetables, employing a marinade or rub with a chile pepper base—Scotch Bonnets to be really authentic. The historically renowned jerk cooking technique—done in earthen pits in Jamaica—was initially introduced by the Cormantee (Kara-manti), West Africans who would become a part of the island's Maroons, guerilla fighters against the British, and later, mercenaries for them in the seventeenth century.

Most people today, from gourmets to fast-food junkies, demand fare with flavor and intrigue. *Island Barbecue* offers some of the best recipes from the vast Caribbean barbecue repertoire. Other recipes are original but reflect an island heritage—an exotic mosaic. Also, to round off a true Caribbean meal, I've offered recipes for breads, vegetables, salads, desserts, and beverages. Bon appétit!

Introduction

**I can vividly recall** the trips that I awaited with some gustatory anticipation as a young boy growing up in Jamaica. My family lived in Kingston, the capital, a bustling metropolis. I was sent to boarding school in my ancestral birthplace, Brown's Town, some 70-odd miles away. The rustic town was cradled in quiet, verdant hills, a winding climb from Discovery Bay where Columbus's party first set foot in 1492. On a clear, star-filled night you could see flickering lights in Cuba from high ground. Most townsfolk thought them to be Havana's, but a quick glance at the atlas revealed to me that they were from Santiago de Cuba, the largest and closest town to Jamaica's north coast.

On my journeys to and from school each semester in Mr. Marston's shiny DeSoto (he was Brown's Town's only limousine driver), there were stops along the route where vendors peddled food to famished travelers. Linstead Market, made famous through calypso lyrics, was the largest and busiest spot, and offered the widest variety of cooked foods and local fruits and vegetables in season. Rival vendors would race to braking cars to sell their pepper-strewn fried fish, peeled and bagged navel oranges—the sweetest and juiciest in the world—roasted peanuts, raw cashews, peeled joints of succulent sugar cane, and an array of other foods. On the journey to school I would only pick at Linstead's comestibles as the real treat was yet to come.

Mount Diablo, or "Devil Mountain," named by the Spanish conquistadors, was my favorite stop then and, as I travel through there today, still is. Eager passengers traveling up the precipitous mountain would soon be rewarded at its zenith. As one's car whined and strained up the alpine slopes and around hairpin turns, behind overloaded

buses and trucks that sometimes had to be braced with rocks to prevent them from rolling backwards, one began to smell and see swirling blue smoke snake alongside the car window. In an instant, as one wondered if the car would make it to the top this time, there it was—a wide, flat clearing in the middle of the mountain, the source of the smoke that now mingled with aromatic wafts of roasting foods nestled on coal pot grills or balanced against burning wood fires. Before the car could come to a full stop, passengers poured out and ran to claim the choicest ear of roasted corn or largest sweet potato.

The roasted roadside fare was as diverse as it was delicious. Breadfruit, corn, green plantains, sweet potatoes, salt fish *(bacalao)*, and local yams, served with canary-yellow slices of just-picked avocado pears, were some of the tasty foods available. Behind the grilling area sat a small cluster of weather-beaten shacks, eerily balanced on stilts, overlooking the slopes of the lush mountainside. In the shacks, which doubled as grocery store, bar, and living quarters for the vendors, were sold soft drinks and other more potent refreshments to wash down the hot, steaming food.

I remember watching, quite intrigued, while the vendors, usually female, with their colorful headwraps and crisp but smoke-dulled aprons, tended the fires. Asked for a roasted ear of corn, they would snatch it from the flames, peel back the blackened husk, and pull it down-

wards to form a kind of ready-made handle—with their bare hands! The salivating customer would then sprinkle salt and pepper on the corn and bathe it in butter. The dexterity of the vendors—peeling back the husk from the corn, scraping a blackened breadfruit or sweet potato—added to the carnival atmosphere, which to a young boy was as much a part of the event as the food itself.

In my youth, the technique of cooking foods over open flames was simply called "roasting." In the vernacular, a barbecue was a raised cement floor, usually found outdoors in the yard, where green coffee beans or pimento (allspice) berries were sun dried. Not until the 1950s when a definite American influence began to pervade the islands did the word *barbecue* become synonymous with roasting. Similarly, barbecuing equipment—hibachis, rotisseries, and kettle grills—are all relatively new to the islands. Besides coal pots and wood fires, much of the household grilling throughout the Caribbean was done for centuries in a "smokeless fireplace"—a hearth stone set in concrete with an area for firewood and a chimney on the other end to evacuate smoke.

The heritage of barbecuing, grilling, or roasting is shared by all cultures, for after the discovery of fire, the earliest way of cooking meat was to suspend it over open flames. Many years after my early introduction to Mount Diablo's roadside grilling industry, I became quite nostalgic while driving through North Carolina's Black Mountain. Much to my surprise, although the roads were much wider, they became increasingly

hilly and winding; sure enough, the air was filled with the waft of smoke and food. To my amazement, the local villagers showcased their specialty—smoked ham—in a fashion similar to my fellow Jamaicans. Alongside the road, vendors raced up to the cars with their hams and whatever else they hawked.

A continent away, in western Africa, I experienced an even more familiar ritual. On the outskirts of Senegal the crackling wood fires were reminiscent of Mount Diablo's. And the fare—corn—was thrown atop the licking flames until the husk blackened. I remember ravenously devouring an ear of corn in what must have been record time, much to the delight of native onlookers who cheered my adept nibbling. They were convinced that my ancestors must have come from that area because of my familiarity with eating the hot, roasted corn—nibbling and juggling with acrobatic skill. Perhaps they were right, as most Africans, on their way to the New World aboard slave ships, embarked from Goree Island, Senegal's infamous port for human cargo.

As a teenager, I looked forward to public holidays, for I got to tag along with my older sister and her friends on some of their picnics. The group, perhaps five carloads of exuberant young adults, usually left Kingston at dawn and headed for the eastern shores of Jamaica, the most famous area for traditional jerk cooking. But the jerk cooking technique was not divulged easily. Some sources suggest

that it was a kind of legacy, passed from generation to generation, the only thing of value to people brought into a new land, forced by circumstances to forge a new culture. As a result, until the late 1950s, jerk cooking was done in near secrecy in the Cockpit country—rugged terrain in Jamaica's interior inhabited by the Maroons—and the bushy hills of Portland, whose capital, Port Antonio, was made famous by Errol Flynn, who maintained a home there. In places like Kingston, the demand for jerked food was so great, however, that restaurateurs with curious monikers

like "Speedy Bird" and "Ronnie Bop" got their weekend supply of jerked pork from these areas and sold it in their gaily painted restaurants to the hordes who waited on lines early on a Friday evening.

My sister's excursions afforded me the opportunity to talk with and observe a handful of "jerk cooks" or "jerk men" who guarded their recipes like some treasure. It was only years after my initial treks, when I pieced together bits of information with oral history and conducted hands-on experimentation, that my understanding of the jerk cooking process finally took shape. Now, as manufacturer of D&H Trade Winds Jamaican Jerk Seasoning, I often wonder if my fate was not sealed from those early days.

If you have ever been to Jamaica and visited any hamlet or famous port—Montego Bay, Ocho Rios, Port Antonio—and even Kingston, you would most certainly treasure one memory. Close your eyes and recall a crowded roadside scene that had you quite perplexed. Then remember the mouth-watering waft of roasting pork, chicken, and fish that aroused your gastronomic curiosity. You were experiencing your first "jerk" attack. And like the multitude of other ravenous patrons, you jockeyed for position on line, impatiently awaiting your turn to enjoy the island's delicacy—jerked food.

In Jamaica, any open space—a sidewalk, a shopping mall—is fair territory to find this delicious food. Some itinerant "jerk men" who cook and peddle their wares fashion makeshift ovens from steel drums; many of these ovens are precariously perched atop wheel-based stands to ensure rapid mobility to better locations. Other "jerk pits" are thatched-hut kitchens-cum-restaurants with ovens constructed of bricks and stones constantly clouded with eye-watering smoke. The spicy, pungent, and tender finger-food is dispensed with alacrity, amidst noisy orders from standing diners. Yes, the jerked food industry is tremendously popular and now rivals rum and reggae as Jamaica's primary endowment.

Although jerk has a rabid following, both locally and abroad, there is confusion as to the word's etymology. Because jerk is a transitive verb, "I jerked a leg of pork" is correct. Jerk can also be used as a noun, as in "May I have another small piece of jerk, please?" And it is definitely used as an adjective in the phrase "jerk seasoning" or in "I could kill for a piece of jerk chicken," which describes the meat the subject craves.

Modern jerking has taken on revolutionary dimensions. Meats of all kinds and cuts, seafood, and vegetables are slathered with a variety of homemade and commercially packaged marinades, sauces, seasonings, and powders—all claiming to be the best and original jerk formula. The discerning jerk "junkie" needs only a favorite condiment and a barbecue grill for indoor or outdoor cooking—or even a conventional oven—to partake of this fabled food.

Much like jerk, the word *barbecue* is not without controversy. It runs a grammatical gamut and encompasses several cooking methods. People in one region of the same country will swear that both their interpretation of the word and their cooking technique are the only true ones. For example, one imagi-

native explanation of the word, adhered to by some American authorities, holds that *barbeque* originated with early French settlers in Florida who roasted whole goats "de barbe en queue" (from beard to tail). I am par-

tial to the Spanish *barbacoa*, which is well documented and pre-dates all other definitions; and, in truth, the word *barbacoa* might have well been borrowed from the Amerindian language.

Over time, barbecue has certainly evolved geographically, and some regions prefer different meats for their grills—beef, pork, chicken, and even goat *(cabrito)*. Also, barbecue sauces and marinades, in varied colors and intensity, ranging from flaming red to molasses black, and from sweet to hell-hot heat—accompany the infinite range of barbecued foods.

Although barbecue means simply "to roast meat," a knowledge of the methods employed to achieve the desired taste and look of the final product is important to truly understand the barbecue aficionado's zeal. Perhaps no other cooking style evokes such strong feelings from its followers. For, wherever you go and meet folks turned on to barbecue, you will not meet more impassioned people.

Barbecue Methods

The Wood Fire

Obviously the most primitive, the wood fire method of cooking meat is almost outdated, for hardly anyone but campers and a few out of necessity bother to gather wood to practice this technique. However, in some parts of the United States, the method—called "log burning"—is adhered to by purists who maintain that only barbecue done with real charcoal—no briquettes here—can be the real thing.

But let me tell you, the best roasted fish that I have ever had was at Jamaica's Old Harbour Bay, on the south coast, in an area known more for its fried fish and bammy (cassava bread). Some of the early morning's catch was roasted right there on the beach by enterprising outdoor restaurateurs, whose pantry consisted of the bare essentials—salt, a bottle of vinegar, varied and sundry unrecognizable spices, and some paper plates. The cooks gathered driftwood, no particular species, and started a bonfire on the firm sand, up from the water's edge. When the wood began smoldering, a wire rack—obviously a converted refrigerator shelf—was placed a few inches above the embers, atop stones, on which scaled and gutted jack and multicolored parrot fish were thrown. When the fish

was sufficiently seared on both sides, it was served with a watery sauce of vinegar, Scotch Bonnet peppers, and pimento berries. To accompany the roasted fish, thick slices of hard dough bread and bammy were available, bought from other beachfront vendors, along with—naturally—the island's famous Red Stripe beer.

There is a special feeling about this simple cooking method, with gentle breezes blowing and the bright sun overhead. Perhaps it's the frontier spirit in all of us, but the wood fire technique of grilling brings out a certain enjoyment—to see an entirely natural cooking process at work.

Grilling

Quick Grilling. When most of us rave about last night's barbecue we actually mean quick-grilled foods, done with little preparation and with anything we can come up with from the refrigerator. Simple, quick grilling is what we do when we come home on a summer's evening, fire up the backyard or porch Weber, grab a beer, and throw on a few half-thawed steaks and hot dogs. We then slather the meats with any handy concoction—commercially bottled or made up on the spot—and settle back to eat, suck up some sun, and guzzle more beer.

Pit Grilling. There are variations to this cooking method that is usually employed for a barbecue party where large portions of meat are cooked. An entire pig or a side of beef would be appropriate for this elaborate preparation. "Open-pit" grilling traditionally calls for digging a hole about 3 to 4 feet wide and deep, then filling it with hardwood for fuel, and finally covering it with sand or gravel, on top of which the meat is placed—wrapped in anything from aluminum foil to banana leaves. Less elaborate pits are constructed with large stones or cinder blocks, stacked 4 or 5 high, to form a square. A fire is then started with hardwood or coals, set in the middle of the square, over which mesh-wire, iron, or green-wood grills sit. The pit is often covered with a sheet of iron to simulate oven-like conditions.

The popular and less complicated method of "closed-pit" grilling is a more familiar technique. The term is a misnomer as closed-pit does not employ a hole in the ground but uses equipment at hand. Closed or covered grilling are more appropriate terms, for the food is placed in an enclosed environment—from a 55-gallon drum furnace to an indoor oven—where, by direct or indirect heat, smoke mingles freely with the food and it is cooked at temperatures of around 350°F. Foods that are closed grilled are usually marinated beforehand to tenderize them and to give a particular flavor from the herbs and spices used in the marinade. Wood chips or liquid smoke like hickory or mesquite, available commercially, are sometimes added to the meats for their aromatic wood flavors.

There is little difference in effect among the various grilling styles except that quick grilling, as the name suggests, can be done in a matter of minutes, while open-pit and covered or closed grilling require more preparation, time, and patience. The essence is that the food is grilled and smokey in taste—something that we all seem to not be able to resist.

Smoking

Smoking (not to be confused with the method of preserving foods) or smoke barbecue, also called "pit barbecue," is a cooking style where large portions of meat are used. After the meat is marinated with a wet rub or dry seasoning, it is placed in an enclosed space and bathed in cool smoke for a long time at low temperatures, between 150 and 220°F. The main heat conductor in this process is the smoke that emanates from a variety of hardwood fires that also lend their distinct flavors to the foods. In the United States, oak, hickory, mesquite, cherry, and maple are some of the popularly known aromatic woods used in smoke barbecue.

In Jamaica, traditional jerk cooking is incomplete without the use of the pimento wood, which gives its unique flavor to true smoked food.

Much of the commercially bought barbecue in the United States undergoes the smoke cooking technique. Whether it be North Carolina pork shoulder, Texas beef brisket, or Kansas City spareribs, the smoking process is used to slowly cook these usually less-than-tender cuts of meat. If you have ever tried cooking a beef brisket, you know how incredibly tough it is. After slow cooking with smoke from mesquite or oak, as the Texans do, this regional delicacy becomes a fork-tender, scrumptious treat.

Rotisserie or Spit Roasting

Rotisserie or spit roasting resembles *barbacoa*, the Amerindian's method of roasting meats on sticks over fire. The modern technique requires a spit to secure and rotate the meat over a fire or other heat source like an electric heating element. A drip pan is needed to catch liquids from the meat. Otherwise, flare-ups will occur, charring the meat instead of cooking it properly.

Whichever method is used to barbecue, it is absolutely essential to use fresh and top-quality foods—from the meat, fish, poultry, and vegetables to the ingredients used in the marinades and sauces. Even grilling, smoking, or roasting will not disguise rancid off-tastes. In fact, unpleasant tastes are intensified with heat.

Barbecue Equipment Needed

Although barbecuing is usually associated with outdoor cooking, many dishes can be barbecued in the oven or on small electric or gas grills indoors. This section specifically deals with basic grill shapes and styles and other equipment needed to grill outdoors. You do not need a great deal of equipment to enjoy grilling, but it is useful to have some items to assist in easier outdoor cooking.

Grills
Kettle-Shaped Grill. This grill is designed for cooking with the lid closed. Its modern design revolutionized outdoor cooking and eliminated the need to control heat by lowering and raising the grill. Because there are neither flare-ups nor uneven heat, searing can be accomplished without charring the food. If coals are positioned to the sides of the kettle and a drip pan placed in the middle, food can also be slow-cooked—the indirect-heat method.

Gas Grill. The new generation of gas grills is equipped with high-tech heat circulation and control. Also, many sport lava rock or porcelain-coated bars that evenly spread heat from the gas burners below and vaporize drippings from the food above. The best thing about the gas grill is that its cooking temperatures can be controlled, much like the kitchen oven's.

The biggest handicap with the gas grill is its inability to effectively burn hardwood chips to get a good smoked flavor. The chips burn quickly and must be constantly replenished. Apart from that, the gas grill is as effective as a charcoal grill.

Open Grill. Not to be confused with open-pit grilling, open grills simply do not have lids, and foods must be covered with anything from a cooking pot lid to aluminum foil. Flare-ups are likely to happen using an open grill, so grill only foods that do not use an oil-based marinade or foods that are low in fat like fish and poultry.

Basting Brush
Most grilled foods require basting, so inexpensive, long-handle basting brushes are a must.

Drip Pan
There are expensive drip pans designed for grills, but any aluminum pan that can fit in your grill is usable. A drip pan is essential for the indirect-heat method of barbecuing larger portions of meats.

Fuels

It's quite a mission to choose from the plethora of competing fuels at your supermarket—mesquite charcoal, old-time charcoal, hardwood charcoal, hardwood-flavored charcoal, "self-lighting" briquettes, chips, and chunks. For briquettes alone, Americans use 25 billion a year, according to the Barbecue Industry Association.

Charcoal Briquettes.

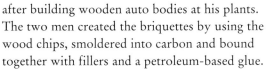

Charcoal briquettes were developed shortly after World War II by Henry Ford and his buddy, Charles Kingsford. The auto magnate was looking for a way to utilize the wood left over after building wooden auto bodies at his plants. The two men created the briquettes by using the wood chips, smoldered into carbon and bound together with fillers and a petroleum-based glue.

Before cooking over briquettes, let the briquettes burn down until they are coated with a layer of gray ash. This means that most of the additives have been burned off. The one drawback with briquettes is that for long, slow cooking, you run the risk of releasing chemical additives on your food by adding new briquettes to the existing fire. This can be remedied by starting your second set of coals in a chimney-style starter (pages 23–24) and then adding them to the grill.

For a fire that lasts for 1 hour, 30 to 40 briquettes are recommended, with 16 to 20 added for each additional hour.

Mesquite Charcoal.

Mesquite hardwood, native to the southwestern United States and Mexico, is becoming the most popular and widely used outdoor cooking fuel across the country. Mesquite charcoal is carbonized under controlled conditions, using no additives or fillers. And because it burns hotter than other hardwoods and briquettes, you use less wood. Also, the high cooking temperatures from mesquite produce a very tasty end-product. Leftover mesquite charcoal, unlike many others, can also be rekindled and used. Use 3 to 4 pounds of mesquite charcoal for 1 hour of cooking and add an additional 2 pounds for each additional hour of cooking.

Other Hardwood Charcoal.

Other hardwoods— oak, hickory, pimento, California manzanita, to name some—are either hard to find or very expensive compared to mesquite. Like mesquite, however, they are carbonized and excellent fuel sources, while also adding their special wood flavors. They are applied to the grill just as mesquite is, 3 to 4 pounds for 1 hour of cooking, with an additional 2 pounds needed for each additional hour of cooking.

Although some hardwoods are difficult to find as fuel sources, the wood chips are much easier to locate. Some grill experts suggest that mesquite charcoal should be used as fuel, and presoaked hardwood chips used as the smoke for flavor source.

Wood Chips. Hickory, oak, alder, mesquite, pimento, maple, and applewood are some of the more popular wood chips used. It is recommended that pieces between ½ to 1 inch thick be selected and soaked for at least 30 minutes before they are added to the grill, so that they smolder rather than act as a heat source.

Herbs
Many cooks are now piling fresh-cut herbs such as thyme, rosemary, marjoram, dill, parsley, and scallions (the green part) on their coals. Dried herbs can also be used. Dampen the herb of choice and add to the coals just before the food is put on the grill.

Grill Brush
The grill brush is essential for proper grill care and is used to brush the grill before oiling and after cooking to prevent food particles or grease build-up.

Mitts
Fireproof mitts are a must for the griller, for you will have a tendency to touch the grill or food with your hands.

Hinged Wire Basket
These baskets are used for holding fish, patties, vegetables, and bread between the grills. Place the food inside and place basket over the heat. When one side of the food is grilled, simply flip it over.

Roast Racks
A V-shaped aluminum or stainless-steel tong-like implement, roast racks hold large pieces of meat or poultry as they cook.

Skewers
Metal and bamboo skewers are the most popular skewers and are essential for kebab recipes. Bamboo skewers should be soaked for 30 minutes before use to prevent burning. Because you can always use the extra room, it's best to purchase longer skewers. With shorter skewers you can sometimes run out of space to add meats or vegetables.

Spatula

Purchase stainless-steel spatulas with long blades. They enable you to turn meats and fish without the possibility of tearing or sticking.

Spray Bottle

Always keep a water-filled spray bottle handy for flare-ups or any emergency.

Thermometer

Instant-read thermometers are best. They give immediate read-outs upon insertion in meats and thus provide accurate cooking temperatures.

Tongs

Tongs allow you to move food and coals around and are as necessary as the grill itself. Purchase the longer, spring-loaded tongs. A few pairs are recommended for foods, and separate ones for coals.

Starting the Fire

There are numerous ways to start a fire in your grill, and some of the traditional ways are dealt with here. Newer, high-tech lighters like jelly starters (lighter fluid concentrated into a gel) are less familiar and, in some cases, require more testing by their manufacturers. Some of these products leave a melted coating on the coals or give unpleasant tastes to the food.

However you start your fire, allow at least 30 minutes for the coals to be ready for grilling your food.

Kindling

Kindling is, perhaps, the most traditional method of lighting the fire for the grill. This is where the cook places newspaper at the bottom of the grill, lights the newspaper, adds some dry kindling, then coals. Because the flames usually go out before the kindling or the coals catch fire, the ritual is often exasperating. Keep on trying. You might use a few newspapers, but eventually it gets going.

Chimney-style Starter

A cylindrical container, the chimney is inexpensive and effective. Its design is simple—vented on one end with a grate near the bottom to set the charcoal on. Simply place a few sheets of crumpled newspapers under the grate, fill it with charcoal, then light the papers.

When the coals are hot, about 15 to 20 minutes, pour and spread them on the bottom of your grill and you're almost ready to grill.

This method of lighting charcoal is the answer to adding additional coals to an already lit grill with food on it. The chimney allows the cook to add hot coals to the grill while grilling for long periods.

Electric Coil Starter

If you are near an electric outlet, this is a sure way of igniting your fire. Just plug the coil in and, presto, in about 10 to 15 minutes your coals should be started. But beware, the coil gets very hot and dangerous if handled improperly.

Lighter Fluid

Another traditional method of igniting charcoal is to pour over lighter fluid and light it. Many people avoid this method, claiming that there are health risks from additives in the fluid or off-tastes that the fluid imparts on the foods. Both fears can be allayed, however, if the coals are allowed to burn for 30 minutes. Never squirt lighter fluid on a burning fire, and be sure to not have any fluid leak on your hands—the flames can easily travel back up to your hands and arms!

How Much Fire, and When Is It Ready?

For an hour's cooking time, 30 to 40 coals are usually sufficient, with 16 to 20 added for each additional hour. But every cook has his or her own idea, so follow your experience and instincts. How many coals are needed also depends on how many people you are cooking for and what meats you are cooking.

To have charcoals ready for grilling takes between 30 and 40 minutes from the time you light the fire. The coals should be covered with a light gray ash and no longer be flaming before you put your food on the grill.

Most grilling recipes call for foods to be cooked over very hot coals, hot coals, or medium-hot coals. Because there is no gauge, like those on a conventional oven, the best judge of the temperature is you. By holding the palm of your hand over the fire, you'll be able to tell how hot your fire is. With a very hot fire, flames will still be visible and so you will not be able to hold

your hand over the grill for more than a few seconds. With a hot fire, the flames would have subsided, but you shouldn't be able to stand the heat for more than 3 to 4 seconds. With medium or moderate heat, you'll be able to hold your hand over the grill for about 5 seconds without much discomfort.

Once you have determined the temperature of your fire, add your wood chips or herbs, put your grill in place, brush it with vegetable oil to prevent your food from sticking, and you're ready to grill.

Tips for Safe and Easy Grilling

~Have all your grilling tools—tongs, spatulas, mitts—at hand.

~Have extra charcoal on hand. You'll never forgive yourself for running out of coals before your meal is cooked.

~Place the grill at its highest point away from the heat source. Keep foods on one side of the grill and coals on the other side.

~Always start with fresh ingredients, especially lean meats.

~Don't grill frozen meat. Allow food to come to room temperature, usually about 30 minutes after removing from the refrigerator.

~Marinades should be cooled before they are applied to foods.

~Remove charred or blackened material from food after you finish cooking.

~Precook meats, then less time is needed to grill.

~Some people suggest that a marinade that food was soaking in might be contaminated, and recommend that it be boiled before it is used for basting or making a sauce.

~Don't put cooked foods on the same plate they were on when raw.

~Do not grill in high winds.

~Do not use gasoline, naphtha, paint thinner, alcohol, or kerosene to ignite charcoal. Use only a specifically labeled lighter fluid, and read the directions carefully.

~Children and pets should never be allowed to wander near the lighted grill.

~Grills should be in a level position. Do not place tabletop grills on glass or combustible surfaces, and grill away from any combustible material.

~Do not wear loose clothing or use fringed towels while using the grill.

~Do not touch grill or heat source to determine heat.

~Turn off gas tanks when not in use.

~Do not remove a hot grate. Discard ashes only after lighted coals have completely died.

~Clean out bottom of the grill so that air can circulate.

~With the exception of fish, or if the recipe specifies, grilled foods are usually allowed to sit to reabsorb their juices before serving.

2.
Sauces
and
Marinades

The **origin of sauces** is lost in history, but cultures have used sauces of all kinds to enhance their dishes throughout time. Some sources have noted that Columbus, on his voyages to the West Indies, found the Carib and Arawak Indians using pepper juice as a flavoring agent. Subsequently, Spanish and Portuguese explorers borrowed the Amerindians' seasoning technique and introduced the *Capsicum annum* plants to many regions of the world. In turn, they developed their own hot sauces.

Classically, sauces can be gravies, relishes, condiment mixes, cold sauces like mayonnaises, or French haute cuisine–type liquids. Some sauces are important parts of a dish, borrowing greatly from the ingredients the food is cooked with and from the resulting pan juices. Other sauces are added to the food while it is being cooked. Still, most are accompaniment to the food—added only after the food is cooked.

In the Caribbean, sauces almost always mean hot and spicy, made with a variety of herbs, spices, and local hot peppers. There are some in this category that are preserved by bottling and others that are thicker—pureéd, then used fresh or cooked. No matter how hot sauces are concocted, however, they have been responsible for spicing up Caribbean cuisine and giving otherwise bland food some peppery intrigue.

The difference between sauces and marinades can be confusing. As a rule, sauces are thicker than marinades and are usually used during or after cooking the food. Of course, the exception is barbecue sauces, which are applied to food before grilling and can also be used as marinades or basting sauces. To add to the confusion, leftover marinades are often made into sauces by adding a thickening agent like flour or cornstarch.

To help clear up the confusion, I turned to an old friend whom I consider an expert on the subject. In his current book, *Marinades,* Jim Tarantino defines a marinade as any liquid, paste, or rub that is applied to meats, fish, or vegetables to add flavor. James also suggests a way to use a marinade as a sauce by first straining the marinade and then warming it over a low heat, adding one to two tablespoons of citrus juice, as well as one to two tablespoons of fresh herb (preferably of the same kind used in the original marinade recipe), and a touch of freshly ground pepper.

However they are used, sauces and marinades are integral components of the grilling techniques, for they both help to tenderize and moisten foods.

Jerk Marinade

Jerk marinades have certainly come a long way since the Maroons hunted wild boar and whipped up a mixture of spices on the spot. At last count there were over twenty different brands of marinades on the market. This recipe is only slightly different from the commercially available D&H Trade Winds Jamaican Jerk Seasoning, which is as close to the traditional formula as you can get. This particular recipe is excellent on chicken, fish, and ribs.

1 teaspoon ground Jamaican pimento (allspice)
1/2 teaspoon ground nutmeg
1/2 teaspoon ground cinnamon
1/2 cup finely chopped scallions (green and
    white parts)
4 Scotch Bonnet peppers or 6 jalapeños, stems
    removed and cut in halves, retaining seeds
1/2 cup distilled white vinegar
1/4 cup soy sauce
2 tablespoons vegetable oil
1 tablespoon salt
Pinch of garlic powder

Combine all the ingredients in a blender or food processor. Process or blend on the liquefy setting for 2 minutes. Pour into a jar and refrigerate until ready for use. Jerk marinade will remain good indefinitely as long as it is covered and kept refrigerated.

The jerk marinade is simple to use. Marinate poultry, fish, and meat for 3 hours or overnight in the refrigerator, brushing on the marinade. I recommend 1 tablespoon to a pound of meat, but for a zestier taste, the cook can use more to taste.

Yield: 1 cup

Jerk Sauce

To transform the Jerk Marinade recipe (above) into a sauce that can be used as a condiment or table sauce, simply pour the liquefied ingredients into a nonreactive saucepan and bring to a boil. Add 1/2 cup of distilled white vinegar, cover, and simmer for 15 minutes, stirring occasionally. Cool at room temperature, pour into a heatproof jar, cover loosely, and refrigerate. (This cooking method is not to be considered traditional canning and thus does not eliminate spoilage microorganisms.) As long as it is refrigerated, the sauce will keep indefinitely. It is used on beef, pork, poultry, and fish.

Yield: about 1 1/2 cups

Jerk Rub

The key ingredients in the rub are the Jamaican pimento and the Scotch Bonnet peppers. Although they are present in the Jerk Marinade recipe (page 31), its consistency is too liquid to accent the sharp, incendiary nature of the peppers and the pimento. The jerk rub is best used on pork and game, thoroughly rubbed on an hour before cooking.

*3/4 cup finely chopped scallions (green and
    white parts)*
1 tablespoon salt
1 teaspoon ground Jamaican pimento (allspice)
1/2 teaspoon ground nutmeg
1/4 teaspoon ground cinnamon
*4 Scotch Bonnet peppers or 6 jalapeños, cut in
    halves, stems removed, retaining seeds*
1 teaspoon freshly ground black pepper

Mix all the ingredients together and mash into a paste in a mortar. Then scrape into a blender or food processor and process or blend at the blend setting for 1 minute. If you need to, add a tablespoon of distilled white vinegar to assist in blending. Stored in a covered jar in the refrigerator, the rub will last for several months.

Yield: about 1 cup

Dry Jerk Seasoning

Dry jerk seasonings are relatively new on the market and are hardly ever used in traditional jerk cooking in Jamaica. I manufacture a commercially available dry seasoning under the D&H Trade Winds Jamaican brand in which dehydrated scallions are used to best approximate the original recipe. Because these are difficult to find outside of manufacturing circles, I've substituted onion powder in the recipe below.

The dry jerk seasoning is just that—a seasoning. It can be used in salads, soups, and on any meats, fish, or poultry, before or after cooking.

1 teaspoon ground Jamaican pimento (allspice)
*1 teaspoon chili powder or 1/2 teaspoon ground
    Scotch Bonnet pepper (see Note)*
1/2 teaspoon ground nutmeg
1/4 teaspoon ground cinnamon
Pinch garlic powder
1 tablespoon salt
1 tablespoon onion powder
1 teaspoon coarsely ground black pepper

Mix all the ingredients together, place in a jar, and shake well. Close tightly and store. Will keep indefinitely in a tightly closed jar.

Yield: about 3 heaping tablespoons

Note: Although ground Scotch Bonnet pepper can be found in gourmet and Caribbean markets throughout the U.S., it is hard to find. Hot pepper powders are available under many names— cayenne, red pepper, or hot pepper powder. All have a kick and add intrigue and fire to this recipe.

Caribbean Pepper Sauce

Perhaps as a legacy of the Carib Indians, who had a pepper sauce before Columbus arrived, each island has many versions of pepper sauce. Like all peoples in tropical climates, islanders have a taste for incendiary food. The sauces can be red, with a tomato base, like the commercially bottled Pickapeppa from Jamaica, or mustard-colored, like Windmill from Barbados. One thing is certain, they are all hot!

This sauce can be used as a condiment on meats and fish or as a seasoning before or during cooking.

½ teaspoon ground Jamaican pimento (allspice)
12 Scotch Bonnet peppers or 18 jalapeños, stems removed and cut in halves, retaining seeds
¼ teaspoon ground achiote (annatto)
½ teaspoon salt
2 medium onions, grated
6 ounces tomato paste
1½ cups distilled white vinegar
½ teaspoon garlic powder

Combine all ingredients in a blender or food processor for 2 minutes. Pour into a saucepan and bring to a boil. Cool, pour into a jar, cover tightly, and refrigerate. If kept covered tightly and refrigerated, the pepper sauce will remain fresh indefinitely.

Yield: about 2½ cups

Rum Barbecue Sauce

This recipe actually has its roots in Southern cooking. I have replaced a few ingredients, rum for bourbon and Pickapeppa brown for Worcestershire sauce, but the results are almost the same—spectacular!

6 ounces tomato paste

⅓ cup dark rum

¼ cup distilled white vinegar

¼ cup molasses

2 medium cloves garlic, crushed

1 tablespoon Jamaican Pickapeppa Sauce (brown)

1 tablespoon low-sodium soy sauce

¼ teaspoon Caribbean Pepper Sauce recipe (page 33) or any hot pepper sauce

Combine all ingredients in a blender or food processor for 2 minutes. Pour into a saucepan and bring to a quick boil (prolonged boiling will caramelize the molasses). Cool, pour into a jar, cover tightly, and refrigerate. If covered tightly and refrigerated, this sauce will remain fresh for months.

Yield: less than 2 cups

Sweet and Sour Barbecue Sauce

A simple recipe using easily obtained tropical ingredients, this sauce is especially good in seafood, poultry, and rib dishes.

½ cup unsweetened pineapple juice

¼ cup tamarind nectar

2 tablespoons freshly squeezed lime juice

2 tablespoons molasses

½ tablespoon Caribbean Pepper Sauce recipe (page 33)

Combine all ingredients in a saucepan and heat, stirring frequently until well blended. Cool, pour into a jar, cover, and refrigerate until ready for use. This sauce will keep for months if kept refrigerated.

Yield: 1 cup

Caribbean Creole Barbecue Sauce

One of my favorite recipes, this sauce uses popular fruits from the Caribbean, mango and tamarind, two of the magical ingredients in Jamaica's world-famous Pickapeppa sauce. Great with beef, pork, and chicken.

¼ cup mango nectar, or ¼ cup mango purée
¼ cup tamarind nectar, or ¼ cup tamarind purée
¼ cup catsup
2 tablespoons distilled white vinegar
2 tablespoons dark brown sugar
1 tablespoon butter
1 tablespoon lime or lemon juice
½ teaspoon salt
1 medium onion, finely grated
Pinch of garlic powder
½ cup water

Combine all ingredients in a saucepan over medium heat, stirring well. Bring to a boil, reduce heat, and simmer for 10 minutes, stirring frequently to avoid burning. Remove from heat. Cool and store in a jar in the refrigerator until ready for use. It will keep indefinitely if kept covered and refrigerated.

Yield: about 1½ cups

Note: Mango and tamarind nectar are widely available in supermarkets under the Goya and Libby labels.

All-Purpose Caribbean Barbecue Sauce

This recipe is from Jamaica, but it's been re-christened Caribbean because I've seen similar ones in other islands. It's good on fish, meat, and poultry.

¼ cup butter or margarine
2 teaspoons dry mustard
1 teaspoon garlic powder
1 tablespoon dark brown sugar
¼ cup catsup
¼ cup Worcestershire sauce
¼ cup distilled white vinegar
¼ cup grated onion
½ teaspoon freshly ground black pepper

Combine all the ingredients in a saucepan and heat until butter or margarine melts. Bring to a quick boil, stirring occasionally. Cool and refrigerate in a tightly covered jar. Sauce will keep for months.

Yield: about 1⅓ cups

Adobo

Loosely defined, adobo is a zesty seasoning mix used extensively in Puerto Rican cooking. If you visit your supermarket, you most likely will see a mixture of garlic powder, salt, and MSG that is commercially marketed as adobo. The native Puerto Rican cook, however, would add tomato—a basic ingredient in most of their sauces—and would make the sauce from scratch, without the MSG.

½ teaspoon chili powder
½ teaspoon garlic powder
½ teaspoon ground oregano
½ teaspoon onion powder
3 tablespoons vegetable oil
6 ounces tomato paste
1 teaspoon salt
½ teaspoon black pepper

Place all the ingredients in a blender or food processor and blend for 1 minute. Pour into a jar and refrigerate until ready for use.

I suggest that the adobo recipe be made and used immediately, as prolonged refrigeration hardens it. This adobo recipe goes well with poultry but can be used with satisfactory results in beef barbecue recipes.

Yield: about 1 cup

Mango Salsa

Commercially bottled salsas now outsell ketchup in the U.S. In the state of Vermont, a place not known for hot foods, there are today a dozen salsa manufacturers. H. J. Heinz has even introduced a "salsa-style ketchup."

The usually chunky relish has recently been popularized in Mexican and southwest cooking, but we from the Islands have been mixing our own batches for decades. Incidentally, roughly translated from Spanish, *salsa* means "spicy sauce."

1 firm, ripe mango, about 1 pound, peeled
and finely chopped
½ medium-sized cucumber, peeled, seeded,
and finely chopped
¼ cup minced fresh cilantro
1 Scotch Bonnet or jalapeño pepper, stem
removed, seeded, and minced
½ cup finely chopped onion
¼ cup fresh tomato, seeded and finely chopped
2 tablespoons distilled white vinegar
1 teaspoon granulated sugar

Combine all ingredients in a bowl and leave at room temperature until ready for use. Excess salsa can be stored in a jar and refrigerated for a few days, but most of the ingredients will become soggy after that.

Yield: about 2½ cups

Trinidadian Curry Sauce

No Caribbean cookbook would be complete without a curry recipe. This recipe was formulated by a colleague, George Marcelle, a Trinidadian, who never fails to impress people with his exotic creations. This curry sauce is particularly good on mutton dishes but, indeed, goes well with any meat, poultry, and fish.

2 tablespoons clarified butter
2 large onions, chopped
½ tablespoon fresh ginger, peeled and minced
1 tablespoon garlic powder
½ cup plain yogurt
1 tablespoon curry powder, any Trinidadian or Jamaican brand
¼ teaspoon salt
½ cup chopped tomato
¾ cup water
¼ cup chopped cilantro

In a large, heavy saucepan, heat butter over medium heat, and add onions. Cook, stirring frequently, until onions begin to turn brown. Pour mixture into a blender or food processor and pureé. Add the ginger, garlic powder, and yogurt to the blender or food processor and blend well. Return mixture to the saucepan and sauté, stirring frequently for 3 minutes. Add the curry powder, salt, tomato, and water and bring to a quick boil. Reduce heat and simmer for 10 minutes, stirring occasionally.

Sprinkle over the cilantro, stir, and remove from heat. Serve immediately. Store no longer than a day or two in the refrigerator.

Yield: 2 cups

Tomato Salsa

This is a very basic salsa that goes well with fish, beef, and poultry dishes.

2 medium-sized ripe tomatoes, finely chopped
1 Scotch Bonnet or jalapeño pepper, stem removed, seeded, and finely chopped
1 small onion, finely chopped
1 teaspoon distilled white vinegar
2 medium cloves garlic, minced
¼ cup chopped cilantro

Combine all ingredients in a dish and toss. Cover and refrigerate until ready for use. It will keep for a few days in the refrigerator, but the tomatoes will start to get limp.

Yield: 1½ cups

3. Poultry and Rabbit

o**ultry**—chicken in particular—and game birds are natural foods for the grill. Although not a very popular meat, rabbit is, according to Weber's Grill Watch Survey, one of the top 10 unusual grilled foods in the U.S. Like poultry, it is delicate in flavor and it grills well with the right marinade and sauce to go with it. Rabbit meat is available usually with a special order to your butcher.

A generation ago, in the Caribbean and elsewhere, chicken and turkey were considered expensive and reserved only for Sunday dinners and holidays. Today, however, all that has changed, and poultry has become the best meat buy on the market.

Poultry is loaded with protein, low in fat and cholesterol, and is easily digested. Unfortunately, for most of us living in urban areas, only mass-produced supermarket chicken and turkey are available—short on flavor and fatty. Some people, especially in the Caribbean, still have home-grown chickens or can buy them in the markets. Called free-range chickens in the U.S., these chickens are corn-bred and are given no antibiotics or growth enhancers, they are better in flavor than those mass-produced. A special order to your butcher will usually get you a free-range chicken. It's more expensive but worth the trouble, as it will be just perfect for grilling—lean and tasty.

Boneless and skinless chicken and turkey breasts were made for the charcoal grill. Again, the breasts will be more expensive but are worth it, for a few good reasons. Foremost is that the thick and fatty skin on some poultry cuts make it almost impossible for marinades to absorb properly. Then, the amount of time and work involved in cleaning and cooking cheaper cuts is really exasperating. Unless your dish specifically calls for skin-on and bone-in, you will be way ahead of the game grilling boneless and skinless poultry breasts.

Quail is, perhaps, the most readily available game bird in the U.S. Just for the novelty of it, if you've never had game birds, it's well worth the effort to grill a few. And if you're still not convinced to try quail, a few Rock Cornish game hens on the grill will certainly liven up any barbecue party.

Jerked Chicken

Over the past 4 years, I estimate that I have personally prepared 20,000 pounds of jerked chicken—at food fairs, for demonstrations, and at the now defunct Martin's Grand Bahama Restaurant on Broadway in New York City, where I was executive chef. Jerked chicken has become the signature dish at restaurants that offer a Caribbean menu and is a favorite of almost everyone who tries it. I feel wonderfully comfortable with this recipe and promise any cook that if you follow the instructions you'll be an instant success at your next barbecue party. In fact, I'm giving two recipes for jerked chicken—one for indoor and one for outdoor cooking.

Oven Jerked Chicken

2 chicken breasts, bone in with skin, cut in halves
6 chicken thighs
6 chicken drumsticks
⅓ cup lime or lemon juice
2 tablespoons liquid hickory smoke or liquid pimento seasoning (see Note)
½ cup Jerk Marinade recipe (page 31)

Preheat oven to 350°F. Wash chicken in lime or lemon juice in a large container. Discard the juice and transfer chicken, without drying, to baking pan(s). Place uncovered in the preheated oven for 20 minutes. Remove from oven and pour off liquids. (This step I learned along the way and I call it "degreasing." In my thinking, the worst thing about eating chicken is tasting the fat under the skin.)

Allow the chicken to cool at room temperature for about 10 minutes, then sprinkle liquid hickory smoke or liquid pimento seasoning over it. Pour the jerk marinade over chicken and completely brush each piece. Cover with foil and refrigerate for at least 3 hours or overnight.

When you are ready to cook the chicken, remove it from the refrigerator and preheat the oven to 425°F. After 5 minutes, place the covered

pans in the oven and cook for 20 minutes. Lower the oven setting to 275°F and cook for another hour, occasionally basting the chicken with the pan juices. Remove the foil and broil for an additional 3 minutes. Take the pans from the oven and cool for 5 minutes. Remove the chicken to a cutting board, reserving the pan juices. With a sharp cleaver, chop the breasts into bite-sized pieces; the thighs and drumsticks, depending on size, can also be chopped. Place chopped chicken in a serving dish and pour the pan juices over. Wait for about 10 minutes for meat to reabsorb the juices before serving.

If you have ever been to Jamaica, you know that Red Stripe beer is the national favorite. It seems almost sacrilegious not to have a cold "Stripe" to extinguish any small fire that might occur—in the mouth, of course! Then, jerk must be accompanied by Jamaican Hard Dough Bread (page 81), a moist-in-the-middle, melt-in-the-mouth must. And guess what? Unless you live on the moon, the beer and bread are available in any large city in the U.S. You need only want to find them. Or bake a batch of hard dough yourself.

Serves 6

Note: Liquid pimento seasoning is available in gourmet stores and Caribbean markets throughout the U.S.

Grilled Jerk Chicken

Follow the ingredient list and preparation steps, and the degreasing and marinating processes used in the Oven Jerked Chicken recipe (pages 41–42). You will need extra Jerk Marinade (page 31), however (which can now be called a "sauce"), in order to baste the chicken during the grilling process. Also, if pimento wood chips are available, eliminate the use of liquid hickory smoke or pimento seasoning and add the chips to the coals. Or, as an adequate substitute for the wood chips, soak whole pimento berries in water for about 15 minutes and then add them to the coals for genuine jerk flavor.

Grill marinated chicken over hot coals, about 6 inches from the heat source. Cover and grill for about an hour, turning occasionally and basting frequently. Thicker pieces of chicken will obviously take longer to cook, so check for doneness before removing from heat. The grilling will leave the chicken drier than the oven-cooked jerk, but chopping the pieces and letting them stand for 10 minutes will allow for reabsorption of the juices. Don't forget the "Stripe" and Jamaican Hard Dough Bread (page 81).

Serves 6

Jerked Chicken Wings

This recipe was developed for Martin's Grand Bahama in New York City, where Buffalo chicken wings were the popular fare for patrons the sports bar section of the restaurant. It was not uncommon for a single patron to devour two dozen wings while watching Monday Night Football. As an added treat, jerked wings were introduced and became an instant hit. They make great appetizers or snack food.

3 pounds chicken wings
½ cup lime or lemon juice
¾ cup Jerk Marinade recipe (page 31)

Use a sharpened cleaver to chop between the wing and leg sections of the chicken wings and separate. Place in a large container, pour over lime or lemon juice, and rinse under cold running water. Pat dry and place the wings in a large nonreactive container. Pour over a half-cup of the jerk marinade and ensure that all the wings are coated. Cover and refrigerate overnight.

Remove marinated wings from the refrigerator 30 minutes before grilling and let stand at room temperature. Place the chicken wings over medium-hot coals and grill for about 15 minutes on one side, turning once. Baste with the remaining marinade and grill for an additional 10 minutes, or until wings are browned to your taste.

Transfer to a serving platter and serve with Jamaican Hard Dough Bread (page 81) and cold Red Stripe beer.

Serves 8 to 10

Grilled Quail

I can remember the anxiety I felt as a young boy as it approached the bird-shooting season in Jamaica. My family weren't "hunters," but some of my friends' fathers were, and it was an adventure going with them to the bush to shoot game birds—teal, ringtail pigeons, bald pates, ground and turtle doves. But that was only half of it! The real treat came in the eating part. Although much of the day's bounty would be put on ice and taken back to be frozen for use throughout the off-shooting season, some of the birds were roasted in the bush. Prior arrangements were always made with a local person, who acted both as guide, to point out the choicest hunting areas, and as cook, to prepare some of the kill. The birds were plucked and gutted on the spot and grilled over wood fires, sometimes wrapped in banana leaves, seasoned and cooked in the hot ashes. Quail is an excellent stand-in for the hard-to-find game birds of my youth.

12 quail
¼ cup lime or lemon juice
2 teaspoons dried thyme
1 teaspoon garlic powder
1 teaspoon onion powder
½ Scotch Bonnet or jalapeño pepper, stem
    removed, seeded, and minced
Salt and freshly ground black pepper to taste
½ cup vegetable oil

Flatten the quail by splitting them up the backbone, using a knife or poultry shears. Place quail skin side up on a chopping board and further flatten with karate-like chops with your hand. Rub the lime or lemon juice in the quail's cavities, and let stand for 5 minutes. In a small bowl combine thyme, garlic, onion, fresh pepper, salt, and black pepper. Rub the seasonings into the birds, inside and out, and baste with the vegetable oil.

Grill quail, skin side up for 5 minutes over hot coals, about 5 inches above the fire. Turn and grill for another 10 minutes, or until birds are golden brown, basting with oil. (Cooking time depends largely on the size of the birds.) Transfer to serving plates and serve warm with Grilled Sweet Potato (page 87) or wild rice.

Serves 6

Sweet and Sour Chicken-Vegetable Kebabs

One of the things I miss from the islands is the ability to go into the backyard and harvest almost any fruit or vegetable needed for a dish. In this recipe, even the chicken could be home-raised.

1 pound boneless, skinless chicken breast, cut into strips
3 tablespoons Sweet and Sour Barbecue Sauce recipe (page 34)
¼ cup vegetable oil
1 medium-sized chayote, peeled, cored, and cut into wedges
1 large red bell pepper, seeded and cut into 1-inch squares
1 large onion, cut into wedges
2 ears corn, cut into 1½-inch chunks

Place chicken in a medium bowl. Combine sauce and oil and pour over chicken. Cover and refrigerate 1 hour. Remove chicken from marinade, reserving marinade. Thread chicken and vegetables alternately on each of six 12-inch skewers. Cover and grill kebabs 5 inches over medium-hot coals for 15 minutes, turning occasionally and basting with the reserved marinade. Transfer to serving plates and serve over a bed of boiled white rice.

Serves 6

Marinated Cornish Hens

For some strange and unexplained reason, Rock Cornish game hens were considered elegant fare in Jamaica. My mother prepared it in the holiday season, and then, only occasionally. But I've come to enjoy the delicate flavor, and charcoal only adds to the hen's superb flavor. Also, if you are preparing a relatively quick and light dish, the hens are perfect, a half bird good for one serving.

3 Rock Cornish game hens, 1½-pounds each
¼ cup lime juice
½ cup olive oil
1½ tablespoons Dry Jerk Seasoning recipe (page 32)

Split the hens in half and flatten with karate-like chops. Rub hens with lime juice and place in a large nonreactive container. Mix together the oil and dry jerk seasoning in a small bowl. Pour mixture over the hens, turning to coat all sides. Cover and refrigerate overnight.

Remove hens from the refrigerator 30 minutes before cooking, reserving the marinade. Grill hens covered, skin side down, for about 10 minutes. Baste with reserved marinade and grill for 15 minutes. Turn again, and grill skin side for an additional 5 minutes for a total cooking time of 30 minutes.

Remove to serving plates and serve with Grilled Plantain (page 87).

Serves 6

Grilled Rabbit with Rum Barbecue Sauce

Rabbit is not as popular in the islands as it was 3 or 4 decades ago, and even then, not many people ate it. I think there was a "Bugs Bunny" syndrome, an affinity factor that was responsible for the trend. As a youngster I raised rabbits and wouldn't eat any from my hutch, so I understand the attachment that one can develop. But for those who do eat rabbit, it grills well and is akin to chicken in taste.

3 pounds rabbit, cut into mouth-size pieces
½ teaspoon dried thyme
½ cup olive oil
1 cup Rum Barbecue Sauce recipe (page 34)
1 teaspoon cornstarch
¼ cup lukewarm water
½ cup chicken broth
1 teaspoon butter
Salt to taste

Place the rabbit pieces in a large, nonreactive bowl. Combine the thyme, olive oil, and sauce and pour it over the rabbit. Cover and marinate overnight, turning the pieces occasionally.

Remove from the refrigerator 30 minutes before grilling. Remove rabbit from the marinade, reserving marinade. Place rabbit over hot coals and grill covered for 35 minutes, basting frequently and turning occasionally.

Transfer rabbit to a serving platter and cover to keep warm.

In a small saucepan combine remainder of marinade with cornstarch that has been dissolved in lukewarm water. Add broth, butter, and salt. Cook over medium heat, stirring constantly until thickened and smooth.

Transfer the rabbit to serving plates and spoon sauce over rabbit in equal proportions. Serve with Island Rice and Peas (page 89) and Island Potpourri Salad (page 91).

Serves 6

Puerto Rican Barbecued Chicken

Everyone has a recipe that they national-ize—like this one, which was so named because it was my first home-cooked barbecue meal on my many trips to Puerto Rico. Back in the late '70s, when I exported onions and pota-toes to Puerto Rico, my business partner, Juan Velasquez, would invite me to dine at his grand-mother's on occasion. Her barbecued chick-en was my favorite. We would sit out in her backyard in the boiling sun and shoot the breeze while she did her thing on a fire-blackened grill, atop a charcoal fire.

3 pounds meaty chicken pieces (breasts, drumsticks)
1 tablespoon lime juice
1 cup Adobo recipe (page 36)

Mix the lime juice with the adobo and brush about a half cup on the chicken pieces. Grill 4 to 5 inches above hot coals, turning as needed to avoid charring and to cook evenly. When the chicken is almost done, brush on the remaining adobo and grill for an additional 5 minutes.

Excellent with a green salad and French bread.

Serves 4

4. Fish

**ish,** according to some sources, is the perfect food. It is high in protein, low in fat, full of flavor, and cooks quickly. And, if the nutritionists and scientists are correct, omega-3, an oil found only in fish, helps reduce cholesterol in humans. What else could you ask for! In almost every Caribbean country that I've visited, it's a wonderful adventure to go to the seaside most any morning and wait to choose your fresh fish right on the spot. From the fisherman's catch, multicolored snapper, silvery-skin "flying fish" in Barbados, grouper and langusta in the Bahamas—they all lie in the bottoms of dugout canoes, just waiting to grace the skillet or grill.

Most tourists to the islands will remember a seafood dish as their most delicious meal. It's not hard to imagine why, as most freshly caught seafood becomes lunch or dinner fare the same day it is caught. And thanks to the growing demand for fish in the U.S., many varieties of seafood, especially from the Caribbean region, are readily available.

If the fish you are buying is fresh, it will have no smell. A fishy smell, a sour smell, or a smell of ammonia signals poor quality, so beware. Look at the fish; fresh fish should have a natural shine, poor quality fish will appear dull and yellowish, and really bad fish will be a brownish color.

If when you touch the fish, it's sticky, get your fish elsewhere. Sticky fish is usually soaked in brine to hide defects. Brine also causes the fish to swell, so you'll be paying for the water content from bloating.

Grilled seafood is on the rise and is indicative of the way we now eat—simple, light, and quickly, with a low fat and caloric intake. It is also flavorful. And if you really want to impress your guests at your next barbecue party, try grilling lobsters or crabs. The only thing that probably would be missing would be the ocean! I tell you, there is no greater feeling than to dig your toes in the sand and pick away at your grilled lobster or crab claws. If you try grilling shellfish, you'll have a hard time getting rid of your guests. Have plenty of tails on hand, for you'll be sure to get requests for "seconds."

Jerked Fish

When the jerk craze took off in Jamaica, every conceivable meat became a candidate for the incendiary barbecue process. Fish has become one of my favorite meats to jerk because its simple to prepare and cooks quickly.

I recommend using easily obtained kingfish steaks for this recipe, primarily because it's a firm fish with very few bones.

6 kingfish steaks, 8 ounces each
½ cup lime or lemon juice
⅓ cup Jerk Marinade recipe (page 31)

Wash steaks in the lime or lemon juice, rinse, and pat dry. Place in a shallow dish and pour the jerk marinade over. Turn steaks so that both sides are well coated.

Remove steaks from the marinade, reserving the marinade. Place the steaks over hot coals and cook them for 5 minutes on each side, basting them with the marinade before turning.

Transfer steaks to serving plates and serve with Jamaican Hard Dough Bread (page 81) and your favorite beverage.

Serves 6

Spicy Barbecued Tuna with Mango Salsa

This is a great dish! The salsa, coconut, and ginger blended together give an exotic flavor.

⅓ cup red cooking wine
¼ cup coconut oil
1 teaspoon powdered ginger
6 tuna steaks, each about 8 ounces and
  ¾-inch thick
Mango Salsa recipe (page 36)

Mix wine, oil, and ginger together and marinate tuna steaks in a shallow dish for 1 hour, turning once. Reserve marinade.

Grill tuna steaks over hot coals for 4 minutes, basting with the reserved marinade. Turn and grill for another 4 minutes or until tuna segments begin to separate.

Transfer tuna to serving plates and spoon equal portions of mango salsa over each steak. Serve with a green salad, Grilled Plantain (page 87), and cold Red Stripe beer.

Serves 6

Grilled Swordfish

The dense, meaty texture of swordfish is remarkably suited for grilling and its flavor is well accented by the wonderful aroma of charcoal.

1½ tablespoons coconut oil
1 tablespoon Caribbean Pepper Sauce recipe
  (page 33)
Salt to taste
1 tablespoon freshly squeezed lime juice
6 swordfish steaks, each about 8 ounces and
  ¾-inch thick

Mix the oil, sauce, salt, and lime juice in a small bowl. Place swordfish steaks in a shallow dish. Spread half of the marinade evenly over the steaks. Turn them and spread the remaining half of the marinade. Let the steaks stand at room temperature for ½ hour.

Grill steaks over hot coals, allowing about 4 minutes on each side, or until the flesh starts to separate. Remove to a serving plate and serve with Stuffed Tomatoes (page 85) and long, cold glasses of Strawberry-flavored Lemonade (page 101).

Serves 6

Jerked Mako Shark

I must confess that this recipe was discovered quite by accident. It was developed on the spur of the moment—in front of over 300 people!

In 1989, I was invited to participate at the Miami Book Fair International, on the Miami-Dade's Wolfson Campus. I was the opening act, on an outdoor stage, with cameras, the press, and the whole nine yards! I was supposed to be demonstrating jerked chicken and an escovitched fish dish (marinated fish), but my sous chef had been unable to find the fish I had requested. Instead, I was supplied with mako shark. Because the pieces were too large and uneven to sauté (which was what my original dish had called for), I had to improvise and do two jerk dishes with different meats. It worked!

4 mako shark steaks, about ½ pound each
  and 1 inch thick
Milk
6 tablespoons Jerk Marinade recipe (page 31)

Because shark sometimes comes with the odor and taste of ammonia, cover the steaks in milk to soak for about 30 minutes. Then wash off the milk in cold water and pat dry. Place the steaks in a nonreactive dish and use two tablespoons of jerk marinade to coat the steaks. Turn the steaks over and use another two tablespoons of marinade to coat. Marinate at room temperature for 1 hour. Place the steaks about 6 inches over hot

coals and cook for 5 minutes on each side or until the flesh starts to separate, brushing on the remaining marinade frequently. Transfer the steaks to plates and serve with the Island Potpourri Salad (page 91) and Jamaican Hard Dough Bread (page 81).

Serves 4

Grilled Red Snapper with Tomato Salsa

I believe that red snapper is, perhaps, everyone's favorite fish. It certainly is a hit in the Caribbean, and is one of my favorites. In developing this dish, I found that red snapper fillets are extremely hard to handle on the grill, for the fish tends to separate very quickly. But it's not impossible and definitely worth it!

1 whole dressed snapper, 4 pounds, head intact
½ cup lemon juice
½ teaspoon dried thyme leaves
Salt and freshly ground black pepper to taste, or 2 teaspoons Dry Jerk Seasoning recipe (page 32)
⅓ cup olive oil
1½ cups Tomato Salsa recipe (page 37)

Rub the inside cavity and outside of the fish with lemon juice. Then rinse under cold water and pat dry, inside and out. Sprinkle cavity with thyme, and sprinkle salt and black pepper or dry jerk seasoning inside and outside of fish.

Coat fish with olive oil and place on the grill over hot coals. Cook each side for 10 minutes or until the flesh begins to separate. Transfer to a serving platter, slice, and serve on individual plates, spooning equal portions of the tomato salsa on top of fish. Serve with a green salad, corn, and Red Stripe beer.

Serves 6

Grilled Shrimp with Sweet and Sour Barbecue Sauce

Shrimp, the most popular seafood in the U.S., is perhaps the easiest and quickest to prepare. But, alas! If your marinade and dipping sauce isn't spectacular, you haven't done the dish justice. The Sweet and Sour Barbecue Sauce is full of flavor and subtle heat. It separates this shrimp dish from all others.

¼ cup coconut oil
1 cup Sweet and Sour Barbecue Sauce recipe
  (page 34)
2 pounds large shrimp, peeled and deveined
  (see Note)

Combine coconut oil and ½ cup Sweet and Sour Barbecue Sauce in a bowl and stir well. Place shrimp in a shallow dish and pour marinade over shrimp. Cover and refrigerate for 2 hours. Remove shrimp from the marinade, and thread on skewers. Grill over hot fire, about 4 inches above the coals, for about 6 minutes, or until they turn pink, brushing on reserved marinade.

Serve hot off the grill with remaining ½ cup of sauce for dipping. Serve with Cheesy Stuffed Chayote (page 88) if dish is to be an entrée.

Serves 6 as entrée

Note: Large shrimp usually come about 30 to the pound. If the dish is to be an entrée, allow 10 shrimp per person, 5 shrimp skewered on two 8-inch skewers. If the dish is to be an appetizer, then you might want to take the shrimp off the skewers and serve them on wooden picks.

Grilled Oysters

I've had grilled oysters in Trinidad and Tobago, and in Nassau at beach parties. For the faint of heart who could never eat these mollusks raw, grilling them should do the trick. Of course, grilled oysters could never suffice as a meal, but they are a good appetizer to a grilled fish main course.

24 unopened oysters
½ cup melted butter
12 lemon wedges
⅓ cup Caribbean Pepper Sauce recipe (page 33)

Scrub oysters thoroughly with a stiff-bristled brush and rinse under cold water.

Over hot coals, arrange the oysters on aluminum foil in which holes have been punched. Grill until the shells pop open. Use an oyster knife, regular knife, or a screwdriver to remove the shallow shell. Serve oyster in the deeper shell. Place them on a serving tray. Place the melted butter, lemon wedges, and pepper sauce in the middle of the tray. Allow 4 oysters per person.

Serves 6

Note: If any oyster is cracked before grilling, discard. Also, if any oyster does not pop open readily with the rest, providing it was put on the grill at the same time, discard.

Grilled Lobster Tails with Rum Barbecue Sauce

This is a dish for island royalty! I have had grilled lobster the length and breadth of the islands—from the Bahamas to the Dutch Caribbean—and the base ingredients used in grilling are quite similar: butter or oil, lemon, salt, and pepper. And that's alright, if you like the ordinary, but I have found that the magic of grilled lobster is in the sauce that's served with it.

The choice of lobster is also important for this dish. The spiny rock lobster also known as langusta in the Caribbean is best, as it has no claws and most of the meat is in its tail. To the connoisseur, this variety of lobster also has the most delicate meat of all the crustaceans.

6 spiny rock lobster tails, 10 ounces each
⅓ cup lime or lemon juice
1 teaspoon salt
1 teaspoon paprika
½ teaspoon dried thyme leaves
⅓ cup softened butter
⅔ cup Rum Barbecue Sauce recipe
(page 34)

To prepare lobster tails for grilling, remove the soft undercover of the lobster and crack the upper shell with a cleaver to flatten the tail.

In a small bowl mix the lime or lemon juice, salt, paprika, and thyme. Brush the tails with the mixture and dot them with the butter. Reserve the marinade.

Place the lobster tails split-side down over hot coals, 4 to 5 inches from the coals, and grill covered for 4 minutes on each side (or until the flesh is opaque), basting frequently with the reserved marinade. The shells will turn orange-red when the tails are cooked.

Transfer the lobster tails to serving plates and serve with the barbecue sauce on the side.

Grilled lobster tails are excellent with grilled potatoes and asparagus spears.

Serves 6

Grilled Crabs with Trinidadian Curry Sauce

This recipe brings back wonderful boyhood memories as "crabbing"—crab hunting and gathering—with friends was an exciting nocturnal adventure. Usually after it rained, crab holes were flooded in the mangrove swamps outside Kingston, leaving the crabs without shelter and prey to young "hunters." Literally hundreds would be caught.

Traditionally, the crabs would be boiled the next day in a designated backyard, in large pots on coal fires. Very few people bothered to grill crabs back then, but the occasional innovative cook would. This recipe is not unusual, as curried crab dishes abound in the islands. The difference here is the surprising flavor that a charcoal fire gives to the crabmeat, which is enhanced also by the curry sauce.

Different varieties of crab are available throughout the U.S., but the two best suited for grilling are the blue crab and the Dungeness, the latter preferable because of its large size.

3 large Dungeness crabs
¼ cup peanut oil
1 small onion, finely chopped
½ teaspoon salt
*2 cups Trinidadian Curry Sauce recipe, heated
   (page 37)*

For the faint of heart, dropping the crabs in boiling water until they die is fine, but know that you will be grilling crabs that are already cooked. For best results on the grill, kill the crabs by striking them hard between the eyes with a hammer. Rinse under cold water, then place them on their backs on a chopping board and split them in halves with a sharp cleaver. Remove the gills and intestines. Rinse again, and cut off the legs. Crack the legs slightly with a hammer, without destroying the meat.

Combine the oil, onion, and salt in a small bowl, crushing the onion with the back of a spoon. Place the crab pieces on the grill, cover, and cook for 3 minutes. Turn and baste with the oil marinade, cover, and cook for another few minutes or until the shells turn a bright pinkish-red.

Transfer the crab to a serving platter and serve the curry sauce as a dipping sauce. Serve with boiled white rice over which the sauce is sprinkled, or try this with some Roti (page 82) to sop up the sauce.

Serves 6

Grilled Scallops in Trinidadian Curry Sauce

Delicious sea scallops are perfect for the skewer, and the taste of charcoal mingled with the curry sauce makes this a special dish.

2 pounds sea scallops
1 teaspoon lemon juice
½ teaspoon salt
Freshly ground black pepper to taste
½ cup melted butter
1 cup Trinidadian Curry Sauce recipe (page 37), heated

Place scallops in a dish, pour over lemon juice, and season with salt and black pepper. Thread scallops on bamboo skewers and brush with some of the melted butter. Reserve unused butter. Grill over hot coals for a total of 5 to 6 minutes, turning skewers and brushing with reserved butter. Transfer to warm serving plates. Serve with steaming boiled white rice with some of the curry sauce sprinkled over and a green salad. Pass around the remainder of the curry sauce as a dipping sauce.

Serves 6

Note: Scallops go cold very quickly. It is recommended that the serving plates be warmed in a 250°F oven before scallops are finished grilling. Have the rice and curry sauce in place to serve as soon as the scallops are ready.

5. Beef

To no one's surprise I'm sure, hamburgers and steaks are the number one and two most popular grilled foods in the U.S., according to Weber's Grill Watch Survey. The trouble is you've got to go far and wide to find grillers who do these two dishes right. Usually, hamburgers and steaks are overdone.

To make delicious, juicy burgers, ground chuck can be used. The most important thing to do is to make the hamburgers not too thick, about ½-inch thick, and grill them over a hot fire, about 4 to 5 inches above the coals. Do not press the patties down while they cook on the grill or else you'll cause flare-ups.

Surprisingly, although much of the grass-land in the islands are used to graze cattle (Black Angus and Herefords in some places, two of the more flavorful breeds of beef cattle), the cuts of meat leave much to be desired. In the islands, steak is usually sautéed or stir fried rather than grilled, but I have been to some bar-becue parties where enormous, California-style barbecue steaks were grilled. We are talking here about dinosaur-size steaks that no one single person is capable of putting away. The host either killed one of his steers or got a side of beef and did his own cutting and dressing. You don't have to go overboard with the size of the steaks. Have

your butcher select steaks about 1-inch thick (your choice of cut here), fresh and bright red in color with the right marbling, and you are off to the races. Some steaks like chuck, flank, and skirt cuts are marinated; others—the more expensive and elegant cuts like club, filet mignon, porterhouse, rib, and shell—usually aren't. Just get your fire going, grill at the right height, and remember that once the steak goes beyond medium done, it toughens and dries out.

Although consumption of red meat is down, almost everyone who eats an occasional steak is drawn to the grill, once that steak starts going and the aroma from the grill becomes overpow-ering. And, of course, don't forget the kebabs. They are easy to cook and truly satisfying. Just chunk your beef, thread on skewers, marinate or brush with a sauce, and you've come up with another favorite beef dish.

Jerked Beef Brisket

Although beef is the favorite meat for grilling in the U.S., its popularity is recent in the Caribbean where beef is not as cheap or as readily available. I have never seen this recipe done in the islands, but I have experimented with it to expand the jerk repertoire. The brisket is an excellent choice when grilling for a large group of people and when the cook has lots of time.

1 beef brisket, 8 to 10 pounds
1½ cups Jerk Marinade recipe (page 31)
1 tablespoon pimento (allspice) berries

Place brisket in a pan and brush it thoroughly with about a half of the jerk marinade and leave at room temperature for about 3 hours. If you've got space in your refrigerator, marinating overnight is an excellent idea.

Build your fire in a covered grill and when it has burned down to hot coals, place a drip pan in the center of the coals. Place the brisket fat side up over the pan, cover the grill and maintain a slow, steady heat. Replenish the fire as necessary, turn brisket as needed to cook evenly, and baste meat every hour or so with some of the remaining marinade. The brisket should be grilled for about 7 to 8 hours, the longer the better. The outside of the brisket will turn black but don't worry, the inside will be juicy.

About a half hour before removing brisket from the grill, sprinkle a tablespoon of pimento berries that have been soaked in water over the hot coals. Remove cover from the grill and brush meat with the rest of the marinade. Place meat on a platter, trim any excess fat, and slice thinly. Serve with Jamaican Hard Dough Bread (page 81) and lots of Red Stripe beer.

Serves 8 to 10

Spiced Grilled Steaks

When I first entered the tropical food import business, I tried to visit every Caribbean island and Central American country in search of exotic foods. One of my favorite spots was Costa Rica. What a country! One of my hosts on my first trip to Limón had a barbecue party in my honor, and the recipe here closely resembles his.

2 tablespoons softened butter
2 tablespoons lime juice
¼ cup Caribbean Pepper Sauce recipe (page 33)
3 pounds round or rump steak, 1 inch thick
2 tablespoons dark rum
Salt to taste
¼ teaspoon ground nutmeg

Mix the butter, lime juice, and pepper sauce together. Marinate the steak at room temperature for 2 hours in the mixture. Drain well, reserving the marinade. Grill meat 3 inches above hot coals until browned, basting meat with some of the reserved marinade. Turn and grill the other side, basting with the remaining marinade and continue to grill to desired doneness. Place the steak on a serving platter, pour over the rum, add salt to taste, and sprinkle over the nutmeg. Slice and serve with bread, corn, and a vegetable salad.

Serves 6

Spicy Jerked Steak

Although the traditional jerked meat is pork, cooks have experimented with all kinds of meats. I had my first experience with jerked steak in Trinidad, where the national foods of choice are myriad curried dishes. Nevertheless, a friend who had worked in Jamaica and had become a jerk "junkie" prepared this dish for me. I have subsequently adapted it to my taste and it's quite delicious. Less expensive cuts of meat like chuck steaks are ideal for this recipe but the choice is yours. Also, chuck steak is greatly flavored when grilled over charcoal, enhanced by the jerk marinade.

6 chuck steaks, about 1 pound each
½ cup Jerk Marinade recipe (page 31)

Place steaks in a nonreactive, shallow dish, add all the marinade, turn and let marinate for 3 hours, turning a few times.

Remove steaks from the marinade, reserving the remaining liquid. Grill above hot coals until well browned, about 8 to 10 minutes. Turn and brown the other side for 6 to 8 minutes.

Transfer steaks to a serving platter and brush with the reserved marinade.

Serve immediately with Grilled Sweet Potato (page 87) and a green salad.

Serves 6

Grilled Beef and Bacon

If you're asking yourself "What's so Caribbean about this?" just wait! I had this meal at a beach party many years ago in Jamaica, and I have tried it many times—outdoors and in a conventional indoor grill—with equal success. The dry jerk seasoning is a new addition, but it works.

1 pound ground sirloin

1 tablespoon grated onion

1 teaspoon Worcestershire sauce

1 tablespoon unseasoned bread crumbs

½ teaspoon Dry Jerk Seasoning recipe (page 32)

3 small onions

6 slices bacon, rolled into rings

6 chicken livers

2 tablespoons melted butter

6 cherry tomatoes

Mix ground sirloin with grated onion, Worcestershire sauce, bread crumbs, and dry jerk seasoning. Roll into 6 balls, and grill over a fire until browned on all sides. Set aside.

Drop onions in boiling water and simmer for 5 minutes. Drain, cool, and slip off the skins. In a skillet sauté the bacon, chicken livers, and onions together in the melted butter until the bacon begins to turn brown and crisp. Set aside to cool.

Grease 3 skewers and thread each alternately with meat ball, bacon, chicken liver, onion, and cherry tomato, using 2 of each ingredient, except for the onion, for each skewer. Reheat over hot coals for about 10 minutes, turning skewers to cook evenly.

Transfer meats and vegetables onto 2 long loaves of Italian bread, cut into sandwiches, and serve with your favorite beverage.

Serves 6

Island Steak Kebabs

I have discovered that necessity is truly the mother of invention. If the cook is daring, with a dash of this and a pinch of that, seemingly familiar dishes can take on a whole new taste. I have tried this recipe on several catering jobs and it went over tremendously well.

2 pounds boneless tender sirloin steaks cut into
    1½-inch cubes
½ pound calf liver, cut into 1-inch cubes
¼ cup vegetable oil
2 tablespoons dark rum
½ teaspoon dried thyme leaves
2 tablespoons minced scallions
12 fresh mushroom caps
12 small onions
1 medium-sized red bell pepper, seeded and
    cut into 1-inch squares
1 medium-sized green bell pepper, seeded and
    cut into 1-inch squares
Salt and freshly ground pepper to taste
½ cup Caribbean Creole Barbecue Sauce recipe
    (page 35) (optional)

In a large mixing bowl combine steak, liver, oil, rum, thyme, and scallions. Mix well, cover, and marinate in the refrigerator for 3 hours.

Simmer mushrooms for about 2 minutes in boiling water. In the same boiling water drop the onions and simmer for 5 minutes. Drain, cool, and slip off the onion skins. Drain steak and

liver, reserving the marinade. Thread 6 skewers, alternating steak, liver, mushroom, onion, and raw peppers.

Grill over hot coals for about 30 minutes, turning to cook evenly, and baste with the reserved marinade. Remove skewers to plates, serving 1 skewer to a person, and brush with creole sauce.

Serve with Jamaican Hard Dough Bread (page 81) and your favorite cold beverage.

Serves 6

Skewered Beef and Shrimp Combo

This is another recipe from my catering company's repertoire, which goes over well every time it's served. We sometimes serve the Caribbean Creole Barbecue Sauce as a dip with the meal.

1 pound beef fillet, cut into 1-inch cubes
1 pound medium-sized shrimp, peeled and deveined
½ cup Caribbean Creole Barbecue Sauce recipe (page 35)
1 medium-sized red bell pepper, seeded and cut into 1-inch squares
1 medium-sized green bell pepper, seeded and cut into 1-inch squares

In a shallow bowl marinate the beef and shrimp in the creole sauce. Cover and refrigerate for 2 hours.

Reserve the marinade and thread beef, shrimp, and pepper cubes on six 8-inch skewers. Grill 3 inches above hot coals, turning regularly, about 8 minutes. Brush with the marinade occasionally.

Remove from grill and serve over boiled white rice.

Serves 6

Spicy Oven-Barbecued Steak

Not all of us are fortunate to have access to outdoor grilling equipment, especially city dwellers. But don't feel left out—this recipe will catch the essence of real barbecue.

2 pounds boneless round steak
1 tablespoon vegetable oil
1 cup Caribbean Creole Barbecue Sauce recipe (page 35)
1 tablespoon Caribbean Pepper Sauce recipe (page 33) or any commercially packaged brand
1 teaspoon hickory or pimento liquid smoke

Trim any excess fat from the steak and cut into serving-size pieces. Heat the vegetable oil in a large skillet and brown steak on both sides. Transfer to a shallow baking dish. In a small bowl combine the barbecue sauce with the pepper sauce and the liquid smoke. Pour over steak, cover, and bake in a preset 350°F oven for 1¼ hours or until tender.

Serve with boiled white rice, Jamaican Hard Dough Bread (page 81), and a green salad.

Serves 4 to 6

Skewered Steak and Vegetables

I remember being at a rented cottage in St. Thomas, Virgin Islands, with a group of vacationers. I was asked to cook something quickly to accommodate unexpected guests. This recipe has been updated, but it worked then and is still a hit.

*2 pounds boneless sirloin steak, cut into
    1-inch cubes*
¼ cup dark rum
¼ cup vegetable oil
*2 tablespoons Caribbean Pepper Sauce recipe
    (page 33) or any commercially packaged
    pepper sauce*
*⅓ cup All-Purpose Caribbean Barbecue Sauce
    recipe (page 35)*
12 small new potatoes, scrubbed
1 green bell pepper cut into 1-inch cubes
1 red bell pepper cut into 1-inch cubes
12 cherry tomatoes

Place steak into a large container and combine with rum, oil, pepper sauce, and barbecue sauce. Cover and refrigerate for 2 hours.

Steam potatoes in a covered steaming basket over boiling water for 10 minutes, or until tender. Cut in halves.

Remove meat from the marinade, reserving marinade. Alternate meat, potatoes, bell peppers, and cherry tomatoes on six 10-inch skewers. Grill over medium coals for 15 minutes or until desired doneness, basting frequently with reserved marinade.

Serve with your favorite beverage.

Serves 6

Spicy Jerk Burgers

As executive chef at the now-defunct Martin's Grand Bahama in New York City, I had the latitude to create as I pleased. The menu was Caribbean, and, boy, did I go wild! Burgers grilled over wood or charcoal are great, and the dry jerk seasoning gives them that extra kick. I tested this recipe at the restaurant and it became one of our best sellers.

2 pounds lean ground beef or chuck
1 tablespoon Dry Jerk Seasoning recipe (page 32)
2 tablespoons grated onion
6 rolls
Lettuce and tomatoes

Combine the lean beef or chuck with the dry jerk seasoning and onion. Shape the meat into 6 patties and grill them 4 to 5 inches above hot coals until browned on both sides, turning frequently for even cooking. Grill about 12 to 15 minutes total for medium doneness. Slice rolls in halves and grill for 1 minute. To serve, place the patties on the buns and add lettuce and tomatoes.

Serves 6

Grilled Hot Pepper Steak

To an island native, the word *pepper* usually invokes thoughts of heat. When I came to the U.S. and had my first pepper steak made with bell peppers, was I disappointed! This recipe is a variation on the theme and it is good. Less tender and inexpensive cuts of steak are great for this dish.

6 rib steaks, 1 pound each
2 tablespoons whole black pepper corns, crushed
¼ cup Caribbean Pepper Sauce recipe (page 33)
2 tablespoons low-sodium soy sauce
2 medium-sized green bell peppers, seeded and julienned

Rub the steaks thoroughly with the crushed black pepper and place them in a shallow dish. Combine the pepper sauce with the soy sauce and pour over the steaks, making sure that both sides of the steaks are well coated.

Marinate the steaks at room temperature for 2 hours. Remove steaks from the marinade, reserving the marinade. Grill steaks above hot coals for 20 minutes for medium doneness, turning occasionally and basting frequently with the marinade. Five minutes before removing the steaks, place the bell peppers on top of the steaks and cover the grill. Transfer to serving platter.

Serve with a green salad and baked potatoes.

Serves 6

6. Pork and Lamb

 **story goes that the pig is like a saint** because he is honored more in death than during his lifetime. That might be true, for pork is the most popular meat in the world. And were it not for religious and dietary constraints, more of this tasty meat would be consumed. The pig, the first animal to be domesticated, is staging a comeback, however, as pig breeding has seen a leaner animal being produced, with the average serving of pork containing only 250 calories.

Compared with other meats, only a few cuts from the pig are ideal for grilling—the loin, from which comes meat for pork chops and kebabs, the ribs, which are retrieved after the loin is boned, and the shoulder and leg portions.

Pork is popular in the islands, and, with the jerked pork craze, especially in Jamaica, its consumption is at an all-time high. Pork is not without its problems, however, as trichinosis, the disease that is passed on to humans by a parasite it carries, is in 10 percent of all the pork in the U.S. Pork must be cooked to an internal temperature of 160°F, according to the U.S.D.A. *Trichinella spiralis,* the parasite, is destroyed at the internal temperature of 137°F, so the U.S.D.A.'s recommendation seems adequate. There should be no pink meat in pork that is properly cooked, so make sure you even surpass the recommended temperatures to be absolutely certain that your dish is safe for eating.

Lamb is not as popular in the islands as is goat or kid, but 3 decades ago, when I migrated to the U.S., it was quite difficult to find goat meat. As a result, lamb or mutton was a good stand-in.

Lamb is one of the most popular grilled meats. It is a staple for shepherds all over the world, who use outdoor wood fires to grill their meats. Lamb's tender meat is ideal for the grill and is absolutely delicious, the charcoal fire enhancing its assertive and unmistakable aroma.

Jerked Pork

The traditional meat of choice for the open-pit jerk process was pork. In fact, the Maroons were so particular, they only jerked meat of the wild boar that had been hunted and killed. If you eat and like pork, the jerk process is for you.

Although I'm supposed to be the jerk "expert" at home, my wife, Helen, has mastered the oven-cooked jerked pork. Whenever there is a social function on her job her co-workers always ask her to prepare this dish.

Jerked pork is best with a rub, but it still has to be enhanced with more herbs and spices for the true flavor to be enjoyed.

4- to 5-pound leg or shoulder of pork
¼ cup lime or lemon juice
1 teaspoon garlic powder
1 teaspoon fresh thyme leaves
1 teaspoon coarsely ground Jamaican pimento (allspice)
¼ cup Jerk Rub recipe (page 32)
¼ cup soy sauce
1 Scotch Bonnet or jalapeño pepper, chopped (to be used when pork is ready to be cooked)

Wash the pork in cold water, rubbing it thoroughly with lime or lemon juice. Rinse and pat dry. Make crisscross incisions on each side of the cut of pork, wide and deep enough to accommodate the tip of a forefinger. In a small bowl, combine the garlic powder, thyme, pimento, and half of the jerk rub. Mix well, then stuff the incisions with the mixture. Whatever is left over, combine with the remainder of the jerk rub and rub over the entire pork. Place the pork in a deep dish and pour the soy sauce over it. Cover and refrigerate overnight or for at least 3 hours. Leave uncovered at room temperature for an hour before cooking. When you are ready to cook, preheat oven to 350°F, then transfer the pork to aluminum foil and stuff the incisions with the chopped Scotch Bonnet or jalapeño pepper. Pour any remaining jerk rub or pepper over the pork and wrap the aluminum foil around it tightly. Place in a baking pan and bake for 4 hours. Remove the foil and bake uncovered for another ½ hour, basting with the pan juices.

Remove the pork from the pan and place on a cutting board. Set aside the pan juices. Hack the pork with a sharp cleaver, as is the fashion for true jerk, and transfer the pieces to a serving platter. Pour the pan juices over the meat and serve with Jamaican Hard Dough Bread (page 81), Island Rice and Peas (page 89), and Island Potpourri Salad (page 91).

Serves 6 to 8

Jerked Lamb

Bill Hasson, who was my mentor in college, and is still a friend after nearly 25 years, was a serious cook. Bill is one of those people who succeeds because of persistency. And so it was with his leg of lamb. I really don't know when he began cooking it, but, by the time we lived in an off-campus house, with some other students, we all looked forward to his Sunday lamb.

A few years ago, while reminiscing about our college days at Bill's annual Memorial Day barbecue party in his Washington, D.C., backyard, the lamb stories began to fly. It was then that I decided to add another meat to the jerk repertoire. Move over Bill, jerked lamb is here!

6- to 7-pound leg of lamb, boned and butterflied
3 cloves garlic, slivered
1 large bay leaf
½ teaspoon dried thyme leaves
½ cup Jerk Marinade recipe (page 31)

Make deep slashes in the flattened out lamb and insert garlic cloves. Place lamb in a large, nonreactive bowl. Crumble bay leaf and add it and the thyme to the jerk marinade. Pour the marinade over the lamb, cover, and marinate overnight, turning 3 or 4 times.

Remove lamb from the refrigerator about 30 minutes prior to grilling. Drain and reserve the marinade.

Grill lamb about 6 inches over medium-hot coals in a covered grill for 1¼ hours with vents left open. Turn every 10 minutes and baste frequently with reserved marinade.

Transfer lamb to a chopping board and let stand for 10 minutes to reabsorb the juices. In the true jerk fashion, using a sharpened cleaver, hack the lamb into bite-size pieces and serve with Jamaican Hard Dough Bread (page 81) and lots of Red Stripe beer.

Serves 6 to 8

Grilled Lamb Chops

Lamb chops are truly one of the tastiest delights that you can grill. The mingling of the charcoal and the flavor of the lamb is exquisite. This recipe is very simple. With the bare minimum of seasonings and a quick sauce, you can have a great meal. The only requirement is that the chops be thick and not be overcooked.

1 large onion, finely chopped
1 fresh thyme sprig, finely chopped
2 cloves garlic, minced
¼ cup low-sodium soy sauce
½ cup olive oil
½ cup dry sherry
½ teaspoon hot pepper sauce
Salt and freshly ground black pepper to taste
6 lamb chops, 1½ inches thick

Combine all the ingredients in a shallow, non-reactive container. Cover and refrigerate overnight.

Drain lamb, reserving the marinade. Grill over medium-hot coals, turning the chops after the first 4 minutes. Turn occasionally for even cooking and baste frequently with the reserved marinade. If you care to make an instant sauce, a few minutes before the lamb chops are done dissolve a tablespoon of cornstarch in lukewarm water. Stir the cornstarch into the remaining marinade and heat in a small saucepan just to the boiling point, stirring constantly. Remove from heat when the desired thickness has been achieved.

Transfer lamb chops to serving plates and spoon over sauce. Serve with boiled white rice and a green salad.

Serves 4 to 6

Barbecued Lamb with Ginger

It's so refreshing to have a barbecue party outdoors with blue skies overhead. That's one of the good things about island life—summer all year round! However, even urban dwellers, as long as there is an oven, can enjoy true barbecue flavor.

Jamaican ginger, one of the best in the world, is difficult to find. Most of the ginger available in the market does not have the pungency of the Jamaican variety. If Jamaican is unavailable, use the smaller ginger root. Usually, the larger the ginger, the less pungent.

4-pound leg of lamb, bone in
2 cloves garlic, slivered
2 ounces ginger root, peeled and slivered
⅓ cup All-Purpose Caribbean Barbecue Sauce recipe (page 35)

Make deep slashes in the lamb and insert garlic and ginger. Place lamb in a deep, ovenproof baking dish and pour over barbecue sauce. Cover and refrigerate overnight.

Remove from refrigerator 30 minutes before cooking. Preheat oven to 375°F, and in the same baking dish used for marinating, roast the lamb for 1½ hours, basting frequently. Add a little water if the sauce begins to thicken or dry out.

When done, transfer to a cutting board and slice. Spoon over pan juices and serve with a green salad and potatoes.

Serves 4 to 6

Lambchi and Boonchi

This catchy-sounding name is from the dialect spoken on the islands of the Dutch Antilles—Aruba, Curaçao, and Bonaire— in the southern Caribbean. *Lambchi,* of course, means lamb, and *boonchi* means yard-long beans. Roughly, the English translation is "skewered lamb and yard-long beans."

3 tablespoons grated onion

1½ tablespoons curry powder

1½ ounces freshly grated ginger root

3 cloves garlic, minced

2 teaspoons salt

½ teaspoon freshly ground black pepper

½ cup lemon juice

⅓ cup peanut oil

2½ pounds lean lamb, cut into 1½-inch cubes

12 slices bacon, halved

24 pineapple cubes, 1 inch each

2 green bell peppers, seeded and cut into 1-inch squares

1 red bell pepper, seeded and cut into 1-inch squares

6 yard-long beans

In a large bowl, combine the onion, curry powder, ginger, garlic, salt, pepper, lemon juice, and oil. Add the lamb, mix thoroughly, and refrigerate overnight.

Drain the lamb, reserving the marinade. Thread each of six 12-inch skewers alternately with lamb, bacon, pineapple, and bell peppers. String the yard-long beans around each skewer and secure the ends by tying. Brush each skewer thoroughly with some of the reserved marinade.

Grill over medium-hot coals for 15 minutes, turning occasionally and basting frequently with reserved marinade. Untie the yard-long beans and slide the entire contents of the skewer onto serving plates. Serve with Roti (page 82) or a rice pilaf and lots of Red Stripe beer.

Serves 6

S C O T C H

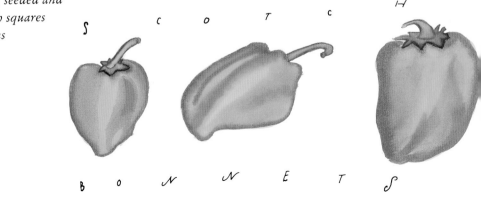

B O N N E T S

74

Oven-Barbecued Leg of Pork

Pork is a popular meat in the Caribbean. It is usually prepared with lots of hot pepper, perhaps because in pre-refrigeration days the peppers were used to "corn" or preserve pork.

5- to 6-pound leg of pork
4 cloves garlic, slivered
½ Scotch Bonnet or jalapeño pepper, stem removed, seeded, and minced
¼ cup vegetable oil
1½ cups Caribbean Creole Barbecue Sauce (page 35)
1 tablespoon cornstarch

Make deep slashes into the leg of pork and insert garlic slivers and minced pepper. Place pork in a large, nonreactive, ovenproof container and pour over oil. Rub in the sauce, cover, and refrigerate overnight.

Remove pork from the refrigerator and leave at room temperature for 30 minutes. Preheat oven to 325°F. Cook the pork covered for about 4 hours, basting it frequently with the pan juices and turning it occasionally.

Transfer pork to a cutting board and keep warm by covering with aluminum foil. Add a few tablespoons of water to the pan juices and stir in the cornstarch. Pour liquid into a saucepan and heat to boiling or until sauce is thick enough. Slice leg of pork and place slices on plates. Spoon sauce over the pork and serve with a green salad and boiled white rice.

Serves 6 to 8

Pork Spareribs with Rum Barbecue Sauce

Sure, you've had spareribs, but not like this! The flavors truly explode, the citrus juice adding a distinctive jab. I've made this dish with the bitter or Seville orange, which is grown in Spain and the Caribbean but, unfortunately, hard to find in the United States. Tangerines or a combination of sweet oranges and limes are a good substitute.

6 pounds pork spareribs
1 cup Rum Barbecue Sauce recipe (page 34)
Juice of 6 large tangerines or 3 oranges and 2 limes

Place the spareribs in a large, shallow, nonreactive container. Pour the sauce and citrus juice over the ribs. Cover and refrigerate overnight.

Remove the ribs from the refrigerator 30 minutes before cooking time, reserving marinade. Grill ribs, covered, for about 35 minutes, or until the ribs are browned to your satisfaction. Baste with the reserved marinade occasionally and turn the ribs frequently for even cooking.

Transfer the ribs to a serving platter and let stand for 5 minutes. Serve with Jamaican Hard Dough Bread (page 81), a green salad, and Red Stripe beer.

Serves 6

Jerked Sausages

Jerked sausage is centuries old, as is the cooking technique itself. Few jerkmen practice sausage-making today, however. If you make your own sausage, mix the dry jerk seasoning in with your meat. You'll not regret it. It's truly delicious.

6 uncooked, mild, Italian sausage links

3 tablespoons vegetable oil

2 tablespoons Dry Jerk Seasoning recipe (page 32)

2 cloves garlic, minced

2 medium green bell peppers, seeded and cut into strips

2 medium red bell peppers, seeded and cut into strips

Cut diagonal slashes ½ inch apart and ¼ inch deep in each sausage. Stuff slashes with equal amounts of dry jerk seasoning. Cover and grill sausages 4 inches over medium coals for 20 to 25 minutes, until no longer pink in center, turning occasionally.

Meanwhile, heat oil in a skillet. Cook onion, garlic, and bell peppers covered for 15 minutes, stirring occasionally, until peppers are soft.

Serve sausages with onion-pepper mixture and Jamaican Hard Dough Bread (page 81).

Serves 6

Jerked Baby Back Ribs

I just happened to be in the Washington, D.C., area on a day when some food tastings were to be done by my company, and stopped by the food demonstrators' kitchen to see how things were going. Was I surprised! If I wasn't stopped, I would have eaten off a good portion of the new test food—jerked baby back ribs! They were oven done, but since that time I've adapted the recipe to the grill with equal success.

6 pounds baby pork back ribs

½ cup Jerk Marinade recipe (page 31)

Pimento wood chips or 1 tablespoon pimento berries (allspice) soaked in water

Place the ribs in a nonreactive, shallow container and pour over the jerk marinade. Marinate for 2 hours at room temperature, turning the ribs 2 or 3 times to ensure that they are completely coated.

When the fire is hot, throw the pimento wood chips or berries over the coals. Place the ribs meat side down on the grill. Cover and cook for 45 minutes, turning occasionally and basting frequently with the marinade.

Transfer the ribs to a cutting board. After letting stand for 5 minutes, cut ribs and place on plates. Serve with Grilled Corn (page 86) and Red Stripe beer.

Serves 6

1. Breads Vegetables and Salads

I can recall as a youngster that every lunch or dinner menu consisted of several courses of food, a direct legacy from the grandiose colonial dining days of the plantocracy. No matter what the meat or fish entrées, the table always had soup and salads and a profusion of tropical bounty—breadfruit, yam, avocado, banana—all comprising a wealth of tastes and served in no particular order, but there to augment a rich, hearty tradition. In this chapter I have included recipes for my favorite breads, vegetables, and salads typical of island fare.

Grillers are discovering that vegetables, like meats and fish, assume a wonderful, new identity when cooked over charcoal. The fire releases natural sugars in vegetables, which then caramelize to give a rich flavor. In fact, my introduction to the grilling or roasting of vegetables goes back to my youth in Jamaica, when it was more common to grill vegetables than meats or fish.

Nonmeat dishes have gained in popularity, as many people have become vegetarians or have cut back on their red meat intake. Traditional grilling of meats, with vegetables as side dishes, is quickly becoming a thing of the past. Vegetables, perhaps three or four, are becoming *the* meal, especially since vegetables have the right texture for the grill and usually take little preparation.

Vegetables also respond to and absorb wood flavors well, so don't be timid when you grill your vegetables. Treat them the way you would meats and fish, except that in most cases you might want to grill over medium-hot coals, preferably in a hinged wire basket, that allows for convenient turning of the vegetables. And since vegetables have no fat and will stick to the grill, it is necessary to marinate or brush them with an oil-based mixture. Also, the griller must vigilantly oversee the cooking of vegetables for even cooking.

O ne of the wonderful things about island living is the ease with which fruits and vegetables can be procured. As a youngster, growing up in the islands, it was always a thrill to go in the yard and pick your own fresh fruits or vegetables. The practice of subsistence farming—growing fruits and vegetables for your family—goes back to the plantation days of the islands. Even today, with urbanization on the rise, most yards have an abundance of fruit trees—coconut, mango, orange, avocado. And vegetable trees and vines—bearing all varieties of sweet and hot peppers, peas, and beans—are ubiquitous.

Jamaican Hard Dough Bread

Hard dough bread is as much a part of the Jamaican culinary scene as french fries are a part of hamburgers in the United States. It's used as a breakfast bread, sandwich bread, or dinner bread.

I'll be honest and tell you that this bread is not easy to make at home. But I've labored hard on this recipe with George Marcelle, a Trinidadian and consummate baker, and it's well worth the effort. (He is a member of my catering staff, and is greatly responsible for this recipe.)

1 package active dry yeast (¼ ounce or 7 grams)
2 cups tepid water
5⅕ to 6 cups unbleached all-purpose flour
¼ cup powdered milk
2 tablespoons sugar
1 teaspoon salt
1 tablespoon lard
Mixture of 2 tablespoons sugar dissolved
    in ½ cup water

In a 6-quart mixing bowl, dissolve the yeast in the tepid water and let stand until bubbles begin to appear. In another bowl combine the flour, powdered milk, sugar, and salt, and work in the lard. In the 6-quart bowl combine the latter mixture with the yeast-water mixture. Knead on a lightly floured surface for 6 to 7 minutes into a stiff dough.

Return the dough to a clean 6-quart mixing bowl and cover with a towel. Let the dough rise in a warm place (about 75°F) for about 1 hour or until double in bulk. Punch down, divide the dough into halves, and shape each into a smooth ball. Cover and let rest for about 10 minutes. Shape into loaves and place into 2 greased 9-inch loaf pans. Cover and let rise in a warm place until doubled, about an hour. Bake in a preheated 375°F oven for 10 minutes. Reduce heat to 350°F and continue to bake for 20 minutes.

Remove from pans, brush the top of the loaves with the sugar-water mixture, and let cool on wire rack. Delicious with almost any island dish, or by itself with butter.

Yield: 2 loaves

Roti

Brought to the islands in the nineteenth century by indentured East Indian laborers, the roti is a natural accompaniment to any barbecue meal. In the Caribbean it is eaten with vegetables, meat, or any number of curry concoctions. It's often served in fast-food restaurants and by mobile vendors just as the hot dog is in America.

The roti is easily prepared on a flat, iron griddle, called a *tawa*, which can be heated over any heat source. Traditionally, it is heated over hot coals. As an alternative method, a member of my catering business, Neil Daniel, a Trinidadian, prepares this bread with much agility and ease using a heavy skillet or a square sheet of iron, about a half-inch thick, placed over the burners of a conventional stove.

The recipe here is simple and fairly easy to prepare. If rotis are to be filled with dollops of meat or vegetable, they are made with a diameter of 12 inches. If they are used as bread to dip in gravies and curries, the diameter is 8 inches.

2 cups all-purpose flour
1 teaspoon baking powder
½ teaspoon salt
3 tablespoons butter or vegetable shortening
½ cup cold water
Flour
½ cup vegetable oil

Sift the flour, baking powder, and salt together in a bowl. With your fingertips, work in the butter or vegetable shortening. Add ¼ cup cold water and knead into a stiff dough. Add the remaining water by tablespoons until the dough holds together, and knead until smooth.

Cover and leave at room temperature for about a half-hour. Knead again for 5 minutes and divide into 4 equal-sized balls. Roll out on a floured board into 12- or 8-inch circles. Brush lightly with vegetable oil and sprinkle with flour. Fold in half, cover, and leave at room temperature for a half-hour.

In the meantime, prepare your *tawa*, griddle, skillet, or sheet of iron and have it heated. Open the folded dough, roll out on a floured board into 12- or 8-inch circles, and, depending on the size of the *tawa*, griddle, skillet, or sheet of iron, cook one or any number of rotis for 1 minute. Turn rotis with a spatula, brush with a thin layer of vegetable oil, and cook for 2 minutes. Brush with a thin layer of vegetable oil, turn again, and cook for about 2 minutes—or when brown flecks appear on the rotis.

Transfer from heat source to a board and pound with the palms of your hands until they become supple. Wrap rotis in a towel to keep warm and moist. Serve with meats, seafood, poultry, and vegetables.

Yield: 4 to 6 servings

Roasted Dumplings

The roasted dumpling is a great alternative or addition to grilled potatoes or bread at your next barbecue party.

1 cup all-purpose flour
¼ teaspoon salt
¾ cup cold water
Flour

Sift the flour and salt together in a bowl. Slowly add enough water to make a stiff dough. Knead on a lightly floured board until smooth. Shape into small balls that fit the palm of one hand, and flatten with the heel of the other hand. Place on the grill over hot coals and keep turning until brown flecks appear all over the dumpling. Doneness can be tested by inserting a knife to see if the inside is cooked. Serve as a bread with any beef, poultry, or fish dish.

Yield: 6 to 9 dumplings

Roasted Breadfruit

I was the happiest person when I checked my personal cooking bible, *Joy of Cooking*, and found a listing for breadfruit, and instructions for cooking it. It is a Caribbean staple and the recipe basic to most islands.

1 mature breadfruit, 2- to 3-pounds, about 10
*   inches in diameter (see Note)*

Remove the breadfruit stem by cutting around it at its base and pulling it away from the fruit. Place the fruit on a grill over hot coals, as close to the fire as possible (it is sometimes placed directly on the hot coals in the islands). Rotate it until the entire fruit is charred, with the skin turning charcoal black. It should cook in about an hour, but insert a knife to see if it is soft and cooked. Remove from the heat source and allow the fruit to cool for about 15 minutes. To peel, place the fruit on a cloth, with one hand holding the top and the other peeling with a knife from the top to the bottom of the fruit. If the skin was charred through, the peeling will leave the fruit uneven. Halve the fruit and remove the heart or core and cut into slices. Place in a serving dish.

The breadfruit can also be baked in a 350°F oven for about an hour and handled in the same manner as the roasted fruit.

Serve with jerked meat, fish, and pork dishes.

Serves 6 to 8

Note: The mature fruit is best for roasting or baking. Mature fruits are usually between 8 and 10 inches in diameter. Younger, smaller fruits are not good for roasting but are boiled and cooked in soups as a vegetable.

Mixed Grilled Vegetables

This is a superb vegetarian dish. I have been accustomed to grilled vegetables since my childhood days in Jamaica, but Americans have stuck, until recently, with "meats only" for the grill. I am happy to report a rise in grilled vegetable recipes.

½ cup olive oil
3 cloves garlic, crushed
2 teaspoons fresh thyme, chopped
2 medium onions, sliced ¼ inch thick
2 small eggplants, halved lengthwise
1 chayote, halved lengthwise, and cored
12 shiitake mushroom caps, halved
2 red, yellow, or green bell peppers, seeded and cut in quarters
6 russet potatoes with skins, sliced ½-inch thick
Salt and freshly ground pepper to taste

Combine oil, garlic, and thyme in a small bowl. Place vegetables in a dish and pour over oil mixture. Marinate at room temperature for 1 hour. Season with salt and pepper and thread 6 skewers, alternating vegetables. Grill over medium coals for 10 minutes, turning vegetables occasionally.

Remove from the skewers, chop eggplants and chayote into chunks, and transfer all the vegetables to a serving platter. Serve warm with any meat dish, or serve alone.

Serves 6

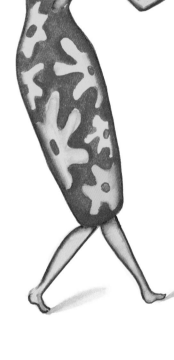

Stuffed Tomatoes

This recipe hails from the kitchen of Ma Chance, a native and renowned restaurateur of St. Martin in the French West Indies. I have expanded on it a bit, but her Creole signature—French and African—remains intact.

6 firm, medium-sized tomatoes
⅓ cup olive oil
1 teaspoon Caribbean Pepper Sauce recipe
    (page 33)
2 tablespoons lemon juice
Salt to taste
½ teaspoon crushed fresh thyme
⅓ cup fresh chopped parsley
1 tablespoon butter
1 large onion, finely chopped
1 large stalk celery, chopped
½ green bell pepper, seeded and finely chopped
⅓ pound small fresh shrimp, peeled and deveined
1 egg lightly beaten
⅔ cup bread crumbs

Horizontally cut off the stem ends of the tomatoes and discard. Remove pulp carefully, without breaking the skins. Mash pulp and set aside. In a large, heavy skillet, heat the olive oil and add the reserved pulp and all the ingredients except the shrimp, egg, and bread crumbs. Sauté, stirring occasionally, until the vegetables are tender. Add the shrimp and egg, and sauté for about 2 minutes. Remove mixture from the skillet and spoon equal parts into the tomato shells. Sprinkle each filled tomato with the bread crumbs.

Preheat oven to 350°F. Place the stuffed tomatoes in a pan with water (a *bain-marie*) to prevent scorching, and bake for 10 minutes.

Serve with meats as a vegetable or alone as a lunch, allowing 2 per person.

Serves 3 to 6

Grilled Corn

Grilled corn is a universal food. Only its preparation and cooking differs from country to country, backyard to backyard. My first experience with what Jamaicans call "roast corn" was atop Mt. Diablo, one of the island's favorite food stops. Here's a simple yet delicious island recipe.

6 ears sweet corn
6 cups water
1 tablespoon salt for water
Salt and freshly ground black pepper to taste
⅓ cup melted butter

Peel some of the husk away from the corn without fully removing it from the base of the cob. Remove the silky threads and immerse corn in salted water. Remove, pat dry, rewrap the corn, and place on grill over medium-hot fire. Grill for about 20 minutes, turning occasionally until the husk is blackened and the kernels have brown specks.

Remove the husks. Season with salt and pepper and brush with butter.

Serves 6

Rose Bud's Roasted Corn

Down the hill from my boarding school was about 2 acres of corn grown by wealthy townsfolk. The handyman who tended the yard was affectionately called "Rose Bud" because of his success with the beautiful gardens. He would invite me and some friends to eat roasted corn prepared in the following way.

6 ears sweet corn, husks removed
6 cups water
3 stalks scallions, white and green part, chopped
1 tablespoon dried thyme
1 Scotch Bonnet or jalapeño pepper, stem
*   removed and minced with seeds intact*
Salt and freshly ground black pepper to taste
2 tablespoons coconut oil

Place corn in water and add all the other ingredients. Soak for 10 minutes and drain corn. Grill corn over medium-hot coals and turn frequently for 15 to 20 minutes.

Serves 6

Note: This is also an excellent recipe for boiled corn. Simply place all the ingredients in a large saucepan and bring to a boil. Reduce heat and simmer for 5 minutes.

Grilled Plantain

Whereas the green plantain is typically fried, I have grilled it. The coals give a new and luscious character to the fruit.

2 large green plantains, peeled and cut into
  ¾-inch diagonal slices
2 cups water
½ teaspoon salt
⅓ cup vegetable oil
2 tablespoons melted butter
½ teaspoon garlic powder

Soak the plantains in salted water for 30 minutes, then drain and pat dry. Heat oil in a heavy skillet over high heat. Add plantains and fry for 2 minutes on each side. Transfer to a board and cover with paper towels. Flatten with the palm of the hand to about half the original thickness.

Remove paper towels. Brush plantains with butter, sprinkle with garlic powder, and grill over medium-hot coals for 5 minutes, turning occasionally. Remove from grill and cover with towel to keep warm and moist. Serve with any meat dish or as a snack.

Serves 6

Grilled Sweet Potato

The Caribbean sweet potato, the truly sweet and starchy boniato, also known to the Spanish as *batata,* has reddish or pink skin and white or purplish flesh. It is truly tasty and a great treat at any barbecue party.

2 pounds sweet potatoes
¼ cup vegetable oil

Scrub sweet potatoes and rinse under cold, running water. Trim the pointed ends and slice lengthwise, crosswise, or into chunks, depending on shape. Brush the exposed flesh with oil. Grill skin-side down over medium-hot coals for 20 minutes, turning when the skin begins to blacken. Scrape off skin, or peel using a sharp knife. Transfer to a serving platter and serve with any beef, fish, or poultry dish.

Serves 6

Cheesy Stuffed Chayote

Until recently, except perhaps for New Orleanean cuisine, the chayote has been a stranger in America. In the islands, however, the chayote has graced soups, stews, and exotic dishes for centuries. This recipe adds a little magic and is a great side dish or main course.

6 large chayotes, 5 to 6 inches long
1 teaspoon salt
3 tablespoons vegetable oil
½ pound lean ground beef
1 small onion, finely chopped
Pinch garlic powder
1 teaspoon hot pepper sauce
1 cup sharp cheddar cheese, shredded
½ cup soft bread crumbs

In a large saucepan, cover and cook chayote in boiling, salted water for 20 minutes. Drain and cool slightly. Cut into halves lengthwise, remove the white-colored core and discard. Scoop out and reserve the fleshy pulp without damaging the shell. Mash the pulp well in a bowl, and set aside.

Heat the oil in a large skillet, add the ground beef, onion, garlic powder, and pepper sauce, and sauté until browned, stirring occasionally. Add the reserved pulp and simmer for 10 minutes.

Spoon the mixture into the shells, and top each with cheese and bread crumbs.

Cut 6 pieces of aluminum foil, 24 by 12 inches, then fold in halves to get 12- by 12-inch squares. Center a stuffed chayote in each square, and wrap the foil around, leaving the top uncovered.

Place chayotes in a large baking dish and broil 6 inches from heat for 5 minutes, or just until cheese is melted. Remove foil and transfer chayote to serving boats. Serve immediately.

Serves 6

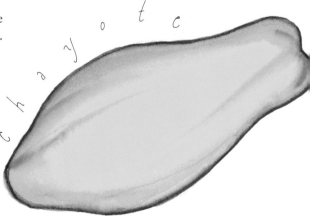

88

Island Rice and Peas

Jamaicans call this dish "rice and peas," while almost everyone else in the Caribbean and elsewhere calls it "peas and rice." Curiously, the peas are what Americans call beans. But one ingredient is universally accepted as being the thing that sets true and traditional rice and peas apart: the coconut. I still remember seeing my mother break open a coconut, extract the meat, grate it, and make coconut "milk" for her traditional Sunday rice and peas dish.

This recipe uses the high-protein pigeon pea, which is just as tasty as the popular kidney bean.

1½ cups dried pigeon peas
1 garlic clove, crushed
4 cups water
Salt to taste
2 cups coconut milk (see Glossary)
Freshly ground black pepper to taste
1 scallion (green and white parts), chopped
1 sprig thyme, fresh or dried
1 small tomato, chopped
1 whole Scotch Bonnet or jalapeño pepper
2 cups uncooked rice

Combine the pigeon peas, garlic, water, and salt in a saucepan. Cook, covered, over medium heat until tender, about 2 hours. Add the rest of ingredients and stir frequently, making sure the pepper does not burst in the process.

Return to a boil, cover, reduce the heat, and simmer for ½ hour, or until all the liquids have been absorbed. Midway through the simmer, remove and discard the pepper. Serve as a side dish.

This is a wonderful vegetarian dish, and I have a friend who perks it up with Jerk Sauce (page 31).

Serves 6 to 8

Chilled Avocado Salad

I've been experimenting with avocados, colloquially called "pears" in the islands, for as long as I can remember. My friends and I would get a fresh loaf of bread or sweet hot cross buns, go to an avocado tree, pick the fruit, slice and peel it, and use it as accompaniment. I still eat "bread and pear" today, much to the amazement of my American-born children who stare, grimace, and use the "yuk" word frequently while I eat my sandwich.

2 medium-sized ripe avocados, sliced
3 small ripe tomatoes, quartered
2 small onions, thinly sliced
1 tablespoon lemon juice
½ teaspoon garlic powder
Salt to taste

Place avocado slices alternately with tomato and onions in a shallow salad dish. Sprinkle over lemon juice, garlic, and salt. Refrigerate for 1 hour. Remove, and serve with any meat or fish dish.

Serves 6

Breadfruit Salad

The breadfruit is a staple in the Caribbean diet that is used in soups and stews. It can be baked, roasted, boiled, and even dressed up to become a pudding. Despite its blandness, it offers many interesting culinary possibilities.

1/4 cup vegetable oil
2 tablespoons distilled white vinegar
Salt and ground black pepper to taste
1 small breadfruit, boiled and thinly sliced
   (see Glossary)
3 hard-cooked eggs, thinly sliced
1 large onion, thinly sliced
1 red bell pepper, seeded and thinly sliced
   into rings
2 tablespoons mayonnaise

Combine oil, vinegar, salt, and pepper in a shallow dish and marinate breadfruit slices for 1 hour, turning over slices once.

Arrange the slices of breadfruit at the bottom of a salad bowl and garnish with eggs, onion, and bell pepper. Refrigerate for 1 hour, remove, and add mayonnaise. Toss, and serve with any meat or fish dish.

Serves 6

Green Mango Salad

I go into the supermarkets today and see the exorbitant prices being asked for mangoes, compared to my boyhood days. Back then, in Jamaica and the rest of the Caribbean, you just chose your tree and proceeded to gather the choicest fruit—for free! Even today, in some islands, it's not uncommon to see this practice continue. The mingling of flavors in this recipe is what sets it apart from the rest.

6 firm, unripe mangoes, about 3 pounds
1 tablespoon lime juice
1 clove garlic, minced
1/4 cup vegetable oil
1 Scotch Bonnet or jalapeño pepper, stem
   removed, seeded, and minced
1 teaspoon minced onion
Salt to taste

Peel mangoes by removing outer skin, then cut lengthwise slices, as close to the pit as possible. Place mangoes in a salad bowl and combine with remainder of ingredients. Toss well and refrigerate for 1 hour. Remove and serve with any meat or fish dish.

Serves 6

Island Potpourri Salad

This recipe was created for a class at the Cooking School of Creative Cooking in Wilmington, Delaware. The salad was a hit even though many students had never heard of some of the more exotic ingredients like the chayote and breadfruit. All were surprised to learn that the green banana, when cooked, is delicious.

12 romaine lettuce leaves
1 medium chayote, cooked and diced
2 scallions, chopped (green and white parts)
2 small carrots, peeled and julienned
4 breadfruit slices, cooked and diced (see Glossary)
2 green bananas, peeled, cooked, and sliced diagonally
1 tablespoon vegetable oil
1 teaspoon distilled white vinegar
1 avocado, peeled and sliced
1 tablespoon lime or lemon juice
1 green bell pepper, seeded and cut in rings
1 red bell pepper, seeded and cut in rings

Arrange lettuce leaves against the sides of a salad bowl. In another bowl toss the chayote, scallions, carrots, breadfruit, and bananas. Place the tossed ingredients in the center of the lettuce leaves and drizzle with the oil and vinegar. Spread out avocado slices on top of the other fruits and vegetables, then sprinkle over the lime or lemon juice. In between avocado slices, place alternate rings of green and red peppers.

Serves 6

Lobster Salad

I grew up having this for lunch at Monty's Inn, one of Kingston's premier food spots and teenage meeting places of the '50s and '60s.

2 teaspoons fresh lime juice
1 teaspoon coconut oil
1 clove garlic, minced
1 small onion, finely chopped
1 tablespoon mayonnaise
Pinch of ground pimento (allspice)
½ teaspoon salt
½ teaspoon freshly ground black pepper
2 cups cooked flaked lobster meat
12 lettuce leaves
3 medium-sized tomatoes, seeded and quartered
1 large cucumber, peeled, seeded, and diagonally sliced

In a small bowl mix lime juice, coconut oil, garlic, onion, mayonnaise, pimento, salt, and pepper. Place lobster meat in a larger bowl and combine with dressing, tossing well. Refrigerate 1 hour. Place 2 lettuce leaves on each salad plate and spoon over lobster salad. Garnish with tomato wedges and cucumber slices.

Serves 6

8. Desserts and Beverages

**W**hen Christopher Columbus sailed past the lush island of Trinidad on his third voyage to the West Indies, he was overcome with emotion as he viewed the trees and plants from the shore. He remarked that every tree ". . . is pleasant to the sight and good for food." He was not far wrong, as fruit trees with exotic tropical bounty are so numerous that one of the most popular desserts on any island is a fruit salad—often made from six or seven fresh fruits.

This chapter is graced with two recipes—the Papaya Custard (page 96) and Grilled Pineapple with Coconut Topping (page 97)—that illustrate how two native island fruits are transformed into simple but tasty dessert treats. Some of the desserts in this chapter are on the sweet side, but islanders are known for their sweet-tooth.

To top off any Caribbean meal, it should be accompanied by one of the region's beverages. Packaged tropical fruit nectars abound in the marketplace, but there is a special feeling when you have prepared your own brew.

The ginger beer, for example, is steeped in culinary history. Every island has its own recipe and tips about how to prepare it. In Jamaica, the chewstick, bundles of bitter sticks from a vine, is integral for that island's traditional ginger beer.

Sorrel drink is another Caribbean favorite. Not to be confused with the North American or European sorrel, the tropical hibiscus is an enigma. Traditionally a Christmas and New Year beverage, the plant blooms only in late November or early December, no matter when it was planted, although the red sepals, which are used to make the delicious drink, take only 6 months to bloom.

As a youngster, gallons of sorrel would be brewed around the time of the holidays, bottled, and served throughout the celebratory period. Every guest had to have some of my mother's rum-laced potion. Today, however, the dried sepals are commercially packaged and are widely available. It is a truly delicious drink, so you don't have to wait for the holidays anymore to imbibe!

Lime Pie

If you lived in the islands you could probably pick your own limes. But don't fear. Limes bought in the supermarket will also do the trick.

1 can (14 ounces) sweetened condensed milk
½ cup freshly squeezed lime juice
1 tablespoon grated lime rind
1 cup frozen whipped topping, thawed
1 baked 9-inch pie crust

Beat milk and lime juice in a large bowl until smooth. Fold in whipped topping and spoon mixture into pie crust. Cover and refrigerate for about 2 hours, or until set.

Serves 6 to 8

Caribbean Fruit Salad

I always looked forward to my mother making this fruit salad. It's a bit sweet, but I've made some adjustments. It's delicious.

3 large ripe bananas, peeled and cut into 1½-inch diagonal slices
1 large seedless grapefruit, peeled and sectioned
1 small papaya, peeled, seeded, and sliced
2 large mangoes, peeled and sliced lengthwise
1 pineapple, peeled, halved, cored, and sliced crosswise
1 tablespoon lime juice
2 tablespoons granulated sugar
½ cup heavy cream

Arrange fruit sections in a large salad bowl, drizzle lime juice, sprinkle over sugar, and top with cream. Chill for ½ hour before serving.

Serves 6 to 8

Papaya Custard

Called a *paw-paw* in the English-speaking Caribbean, the papaya is a favorite fruit that is usually eaten fresh but also used extensively in desserts and condiments.

3 cups papaya purée
1 cup Grated Coconut recipe (see Glossary)
1 cup heavy cream
¾ cup milk
½ teaspoon vanilla extract
3 eggs, beaten
Pinch of salt
4 tablespoons confectioner's sugar
½ teaspoon grated lemon zest

Combine the papaya purée with the grated coconut and pour into a buttered baking dish. In a saucepan, heat cream, milk, and vanilla extract until bubbles appear. Pour warm liquid into mixing bowl and combine with the eggs, salt, and sugar. Pour the mixture on top of the papaya-coconut mixture and sprinkle with the grated lemon zest.

In a preheated 375°F oven, place the baking dish in a pan with hot water (a *bain-marie*) and bake for about 30 minutes, or until custard sets. Remove from the oven, cool, and serve.

Serves 4 to 6

Chocolate Pudding

This recipe is from Barbados, where it is also called "Pitch Lake Pudding," a direct reference to Trinidad's Pitch Lake. It's really good, especially for parties.

1 cup unsweetened cocoa
1 tablespoon butter
1 cup sugar
1 tablespoon unflavored gelatin
¼ cup hot water
7 eggs, separated
2 tablespoons dark rum
1 cup heavy cream

Cook the cocoa, butter, and sugar in the top of a double boiler, stirring constantly until sugar is dissolved. Dissolve the gelatin in the hot water and add to the cocoa mixture. Beat the egg yolks and add to the cocoa mixture. Stir and cook for 3 minutes. Remove from heat and stir in the rum. Beat the egg whites until stiff. Fold into the cocoa mixture and pour into a serving bowl. Refrigerate for at least 6 hours, or preferably overnight.

Before serving, whip the cream until stiff and spoon over.

Serves 6 to 8

Grilled Pineapple with Coconut Topping

I picked up this recipe in **New York** City, would you believe! But it's truly island fare and will be a welcome dessert at your next barbecue party.

1 ripe medium-sized pineapple
2 tablespoons dark rum
1 teaspoon granulated sugar
½ cup frozen whipped topping, thawed, or whipped cream
¼ cup shredded coconut (see Glossary)

Peel pineapple and cut crosswise into 6 slices. Drizzle rum over and sprinkle with sugar.

Cover and grill pineapple 6 inches from medium coals for 10 minutes, turning once. Top with whipped topping and sprinkle with shredded coconut.

Serves 6

Coffee Rum

Two of Jamaica's famous products are combined to create this wonderful drink. If you're lucky, you might find the Blue Mountain brand coffee and Appleton Gold rum, both from Jamaica. If not, any substitutes will suffice.

8 teaspoons Blue Mountain instant coffee
½ cup boiling water
2 cups cold water
⅔ cup sweetened condensed milk
½ cup Appleton Gold rum
Shaved ice

Dissolve the coffee in the boiling water and mix with the cold water. Stir in the condensed milk and add the rum. Stir well and pour over shaved ice in tall glasses.

Serves 6 to 8

Ginger Beer

Ginger beer is one of those brews that is as old as the history of the islands. Everyone loves it and has a recipe handed down from a great-grandmother, and swears that theirs is the best and original formula. So popular is the ginger beer drink that several companies have packaged it commercially, adding carbonation. But nothing beats the home brew. And it's simple to make.

1 cup grated fresh ginger
2 tablespoons lime juice
2 cups brown sugar
1 quart boiling water
2 teaspoons active dry yeast
½ cup lukewarm water

In a large bowl, preferably earthenware, combine the ginger, lime juice, and sugar. Pour in the boiling water and stir well. In a smaller bowl, mix the yeast in the water. Let stand until it begins to bubble. When the yeast dissolves, pour into the ginger mixture.

Cover the bowl and leave at room temperature for a day. Strain, transfer to a bottle, and refrigerate. It will stay good for a week in the refrigerator before going flat. Ginger beer has a sting to it, but it's a refreshing, exotic drink. Serve icy cold at an outdoor barbecue party.

Yield: about 1¼ quarts

Fruit Daiquiri

Daiquiris are popular drinks in the islands and the fruit daiquiri is truly exquisite.

6 ounces light rum
3 teaspoons lime juice
3 tablespoons fine, granulated sugar
½ cup maraschino cherries, stems removed
Dash Angostura bitters
Cracked ice

Pour all the ingredients into an electric blender and liquefy. Pour over cracked ice in cocktail glasses and serve.

Serves 6

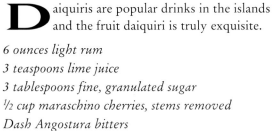

Caribbean Fruit Punch

The ingredients in this beverage are blended, yet each is distinct to the tastebuds. Here again we see the use of locally grown fruits in a tantalizing island drink.

1 can, 19-ounces, mango nectar (see Note)
2 cups unsweetened pineapple juice
2 cups freshly squeezed orange juice
1/2 cup lime juice
Shaved ice
6 teaspoons strawberry-flavored syrup
Chopped fresh pineapple, orange slices, and ripe banana slices cut diagonally for garnish

Combine mango, pineapple juice, orange juice, and lime juice in a blender or food processor and blend well. Pour mixture over shaved ice in 6 tall glasses and add 1 teaspoon strawberry-flavored syrup to each glass. Garnish glasses with pineapple, orange, and banana slices.

Serves 6

Note: Mango nectar, especially from Jamaica, abounds in Caribbean markets throughout the U.S.

Creole Fruit Punch

This recipe from the French Caribbean is well worth the effort.

2 cups orange juice
2 tablespoons lime juice
1 can (12 ounces) passion fruit nectar
1/2 cup strawberry-flavored syrup
2 cups water
Dash of Angostura bitters
Crushed ice
6 orange wedges for garnish

Combine orange juice, lime juice, passion fruit nectar, syrup, water, and bitters in a blender and blend well. Pour over crushed ice and garnish glasses with orange wedges.

Serves 6

Strawberry-flavored Lemonade

I have never quite understood why islanders developed such a taste for strawberry-flavored syrups, especially since the fruit is not cultivated in large quantities in the tropics. Perhaps, as in Jamaica, it's because strawberry-flavored syrup is an integral ingredient in the island's rum punch. Whatever the reason, there are scores of different brands of syrups. In the U.S., even Hershey's, the king of chocolate syrup, has gotten into the act and now produces a strawberry-flavored syrup. This recipe is really good and is a sure-fire hit for hot days and hot foods.

1½ cups strawberry-flavored syrup
6 cups cold water
⅓ cup freshly squeezed lemon juice
Ice cubes

In a large bowl mix syrup, water, and lemon juice together. Stir well. Pour into a pitcher, add ice, and keep refrigerated until ready for use. Great with any meal or simply as a thirst quencher.

Yield: approximately 1 quart

Caribbean Sorrel Drink

Not to be confused with North American or European Sorrel, Caribbean Sorrel is a tropical flower found throughout the region. It can be enjoyed year-round since the dried sepals are widely available in Caribbean markets throughout the U.S. Traditional sorrel drink is made from the fresh sepals, which are available in Caribbean markets in the U.S. in late November and early December. Also see glossary page 107.

1 packet, 1½ ounces, dried sorrel
2 ounces fresh ginger, peeled and slivered
4 large limes, halved
1 teaspoon Jamaican pimento or
  ½ teaspoon cloves
2 quarts boiling water
2½ cups dark brown sugar
¼ cup Jamaican overproof white rum (optional)

Place the dried sorrel in a large, nonreactive container. Add the ginger and juice the limes, leaving the rinds in. Add the pimento or cloves, and pour over boiling water. Cover, store in a cool place, and steep overnight.

Strain the liquid through cheesecloth into a pitcher and discard the solids. Sweeten with sugar and add the rum, which can be omitted if you're a teetotaler, but the brew will lack punch. Chill and serve over cracked ice.

Yield: about 2¼ quarts

Glossary

Avocado, *Persea americana,* is colloquially called pear in some islands because of its pear-like shape. Also called alligator pear, aguacate, midshipman's butter, and poorman's butter in different parts of the Caribbean. A native of Central America, the avocado was first cultivated in Mexico, as far back as 7000 B.C. Avocados can vary in shape and size, and can be a green, purplish, or brownish color. When the fruit is ripe, the flesh yields to the pressure of a thumb. The flesh is a light yellow and is used in spreads, sauces, salads, or as accompaniment to many dishes.

To Prepare: Make lengthwise cuts with a sharp knife around the fruit, getting about 4 or 5 slices, depending on the size of the fruit. Peel off the skin by using the fingertips to separate the skin from the flesh. Discard seed and remove any residue from the seed that attaches itself to the flesh.

Banana. Both green and ripe bananas are eaten in the Caribbean. When green, the banana is used as a vegetable and is boiled, mashed, creamed, fried, and made into porridge or dumplings. Bananas can be used as a substitute for the less widely available plantain. See Plantain (page 106) for instructions on peeling and cooking green bananas.

Bitter or Seville Orange, also called sour orange, is grown in Spain and in the Caribbean. It looks much like a sweet orange but the pulp is too sour and acidy to be eaten. The juice is used in cooking, and the pulp is used to make marmalade. It is sometimes available in Caribbean markets.

Breadfruit, *Artocarpus communis,* was introduced to Jamaica in 1793 by Captain William Bligh of the ill-fated Bounty. Round or oblong, the breadfruit has a green, bumpy skin. It is usually between 8 to 10 inches in diameter and is peeled and boiled like a potato, added to soups, or roasted in its skin and peeled. Its cream-colored flesh has the flavor and texture of bread when roasted. It is widely available in Caribbean markets in the U.S.

To Prepare: For boiling, peel the skin from the breadfruit and cut the fruit in halves, lengthwise. Core and slice. For roasting, leave the skin on, and when fruit is cooked, scrape off the blackened exterior. Cut in halves lengthwise, core, and slice.

Chayote, *Sechium edule,* is also called christophene, bironne, and cho-cho. A pale green, pear-shaped summer squash, the chayote has a furrowed and prickly exterior. It is added to soups and stews, and is stuffed, baked, and grilled. It is also added to commercially packaged pickles. It is widely available throughout the U.S.

Chewstick, *Gouania lupuloides,* is a bitter vine. The sticks are bundled and sold in local produce markets in Jamaica. An ingredient in that island's ginger beer, chewsticks are also used to rub and whiten the teeth. It has been added to commercially packaged toothpaste.

Chive, *Allium schoenoprasum,* also called cive, is from the onion family and is the smallest and mildest of the species. Used extensively in Trinidad and Tobago cuisine, it is also used in French cooking as a seasoning.

Cilantro, *Coriandrum sativum,* is also called coriander, Chinese parsley, shaddo beni, and culantro. It is an aromatic herb that resembles flat-leaf parsley, but it has a more pungent flavor. It is sold in bunches and used extensively in Trinidad and Tobago cuisine. It can be found in Caribbean markets in the U.S.

Coconut. Usually found growing along the coastline of most islands, the majestic palm is not only beautiful, it contributes to many economies with its by-products. Coconuts supply food and oil for cooking, making soaps, margarines, and cosmetics. The long, sturdy leaves are used for making mats, roofing, hats, bags, and many novelty items, especially for the tourist trade. Even the wood from the coconut tree trunk is now being used in furniture manufacturing.

Packaged coconut products are widely available throughout the U.S. Among the many products are canned coconut cream for desserts and cooking, frozen coconut cream, shredded coconut, and coconut oil.

But, if you like to do your cooking from scratch, here are some pointers excerpted from *Island Cooking: Recipes from the Caribbean:*

To open a coconut, place the coconut, eyes down, on a solid surface and crack with a hammer several times. Pry the meat loose from the shell with a blunt knife. If the recipe calls for white meat only (as in shredding), pare off the brown skin with a swivel-blade peeler or a knife. If you are making milk or cream, it is not necessary to peel the coconut.

Coconut Water. Excellent as a mixer with rum. Simply pierce the eyes (black spots at the end of the nut) with an ice pick and drain the liquid. Smell before using: sometimes the water is rancid, which does not affect the meat. As long as the meat is white and firm it can be used for shredding and milk or cream extraction, but rancid coconut water should be discarded.

Coconut Milk. Cut the meat into small pieces and grate in a food processor or an electric blender. Moisten with the coconut water or plain hot water, then liquefy until as fine as possible. Pour boiling water on the liquefied coconut and let it stand in a bowl for 30 minutes. Then pass through a cheesecloth or sieve to separate the milk from the solids. Discard the solids.

There is no hard and fast rule governing the amount of coconut meat to use per cup of coconut milk. Generally a half a coconut will yield up to 4 cups of a mildly flavored coconut milk, or 2 cups of rich coconut milk. Use as much boiling water as necessary to make the amount of coconut milk required in the recipe (i.e., if the recipe calls for 2 cups coconut milk, pour 2 cups of boiling water over the liquefied coconut). For very rich milk, squeeze the liquefied coconut through dampened cheesecloth or press it through a fine sieve, catching the extracted milk in a bowl. Do not pour boiling water over it.

Coconut Cream. Pour rich, undiluted coconut milk into a bowl and allow to stand for at least 4 hours, preferably overnight, in a cool place or in a refrigerator, until a thick cream rises to the top. Skim off and use the cream as needed.

Coconut Oil. Pour rich, undiluted coconut milk into a saucepan and bring to a boil. Reduce the heat and simmer until the water from the milk evaporates. Skim off the cream and you will be left with the oil. Strain and bottle.

Grated Coconut. Peel and discard the brown skin. Then grate the white flesh with a hand-held grater or in an electric blender or food processor. The brown skin can be left on if white coconut is not required.

Shredded Coconut. Peel and discard the brown skin from the flesh and shred as you would carrots.

Curry. A mixture of herbs and spices, curry powder was introduced to the West Indies by the British, who brought it to the islands from India. It was later brought by East Indians who came to the Caribbean as indentured servants in the nineteenth century. Curry powder is widely used, but very few cooks make their own today. Commercially packaged curry powders are available but vary greatly in taste, although most have some basic ingredients—coriander, turmeric, fenugreek, and pepper. Curry powders are available throughout the U.S.

Escovitch, also called escabeche, means "pickled." The technique was introduced to the Caribbean by the Portuguese and Spanish as a way to preserve fish and poultry. In the Jamaican version, the fish is fried and pickled in a vinegar-pepper marinade.

Game Birds. Wild duck, teal, plover, quail, baldpate, ringtail pigeons, ground and turtle doves are some of the game birds found in the Caribbean. In recent years, due to a decline in the bird population, the game bird shooting season has been reduced or curtailed in many countries. The birds are usually roasted, grilled, and fricasseed.

Ginger Root, *Zingiber officinale,* is a perennial herbaceous plant. Ginger was introduced to the Caribbean from Asia by the Spanish. Jamaica produces the finest ginger in the world, and the exported powder and dried ginger are used in drinks and as a spice for pastry and cakes. It is used green in ginger beer and as a seasoning in cooking. Ginger is widely available in the U.S.

Langusta, also called langouste, is the clawless, spiny lobster found in Caribbean waters. It is prized for the meat in its tail and is available in the U.S.

Mako Shark. A highly prized table fish, the mako shark and other varieties of shark are quickly becoming a popular fish in the U.S. Its flesh is firm, meaty, and low in fat. It is excellent for grilling.

Mango, *Mangifera indica,* is a common fruit in the Caribbean. When it is ripe, its skin is pinkish, red, or yellowish and flecked with black and brown spots. There are numerous varieties, but all have succulent, yellowish-orange flesh surrounding a single, large seed. The mango is used mainly in salads when ripe, or eaten as a fruit. The unripe fruit is used in chutneys and salads. The mango is widely available in the U.S.

Maroons. Descendants of African peoples. Some Maroons were runaway slaves in Jamaica, who escaped periodically and inhabited mountainous enclaves in the steep Blue Mountains and the rugged Cockpit country. The name *Maroon* is from the Spanish word *cimarron,* meaning wild or untamed.

Perhaps one of the greatest legacies of the Maroons is their culinary contribution, for it was their pit-cooking style, brought from Africa, that greatly enhanced the spicy seasoning of the Arawak Indians to give us the jerk technique.

Nutmeg, *Myristica fragrans,* is a brown oval seed. The nutmeg tree from which it comes flourishes on the island of Grenada. Nutmeg is a fragrant spice that is usually used in its ground form as a flavoring for foods. It is widely available in the U.S.

Papaya, *Carica papaya,* is also called paw-paw and papaw. A native Caribbean fruit, the papaya is now enjoying tremendous popularity as a table fruit in the U.S. The ripe papaya is eaten as a fruit, while the green, unripe fruit is used in chutneys and other condiments. The papaya is widely available throughout the U.S.

Peppers, *Capsicum* **spp.** A native of the New World, the word *pepper,* different from black peppercorn, encompasses an array of varieties including sweet bell peppers, pimento, red peppers, paprika, jalapeño, and chile peppers, among scores of others. The favorite hot pepper in Jamaica, and much of the English-speaking Caribbean, is the Scotch Bonnet, a tam-o'-shanter shaped pepper, known as the habañero in southwestern U.S. cooking. One of the hottest peppers in the world, it is quite flavorful and is used frequently in island cooking. It is a base for many commercially bottled hot pepper sauces. It is available in Caribbean markets in the U.S.

Pickapeppa. The brand name of Jamaica's world-renowned hot sauces, which are available in two varieties: Pickapeppa brown, which consists of mango, tamarind, and a multitude of spices, and Pickapeppa red, a fiery table sauce. Both use the Scotch Bonnet pepper in their formulas. They are available throughout the U.S.

Pigeon Peas, *Cajanus cajan,* are also called congo peas, gungo, goongoo peas, and gandules in Spanish countries when young and green. A small, round pea, it is also used when mature and dry, when it is called grandures in Spanish countries. It is used extensively in cooking in all Caribbean countries—in soups, stews, rice and peas dishes, and dumplings. It is widely available throughout the U.S.

Pimento, *Pimenta officinalis,* is also called Jamaica pepper and allspice, as it tastes and smells like a combination of nutmeg, cinnamon, and cloves. The Jamaican pimento is world famous, but the evergreen tree from which pimento berries come are found throughout Central America. The pimento, or allspice, is used throughout the world in pickles, marinades, and medicines, and is used as a seasoning in cooking. It is one of the ingredients in Jamaican jerk seasoning, and its wood-smoke flavor lends a unique flavor to jerked foods. Use of the pimento berry as a seasoning by the Arawak Indians predates Columbus's discovery of the New World. Allspice is available throughout the U.S. Its wood chips or leaves are sometimes found in Jamaican markets.

Pineapple, *Annas comosus,* is found in abundance throughout the Caribbean. Columbus came across pineapples in 1493 on the island of Guadeloupe, where they were called *annas* by the Carib Indians. He rechristened them *la piña de las Indias,* the pine of the Indies, because they resembled "green pine cones." The pineapple is eaten as a fruit by itself and is used in desserts, fruit salads,

beverages, and in baking. It is widely available throughout the U.S.

Plantain, *Musa sp.,* fruit of the banana family, is larger than a banana but not as sweet when ripe. It must be cooked to be edible. It is fried, boiled, baked, grilled, or roasted.

To Prepare: Wash the plantain or green banana and cut off about ¼ inch from the ends of the fruit. Slit the skin lengthwise on opposite sides of the fruit without damaging the pulp. If you prefer to cook it without the skin, remove the skin gently with your fingers, using a knife to ease it off. Place in salted cold water, bring to a boil, and cook banana for 20 minutes (30 minutes for plantain) or until the skin begins to separate from the fruit. The fruit is cooked when a knife can penetrate it easily.

The banana and plantain can be grilled or roasted with or without the skin. Green bananas, and to a lesser extent plantains, are available widely throughout the U.S.

Roti. A flat, unleavened bread, or paratha, the roti was introduced to the Caribbean with the wave of indentured East Indian laborers in the nineteenth century. Of course, the roti has been West Indianized, and has taken interesting culinary detours. This bread is now the pocket for dollops of curried dishes, puréed peas, and innumerable other accompanying delights. In Trinidad and Tobago the roti is what hamburgers are to the U.S. Roti shops—fast food restaurants—serving this delightful finger food, have sprung up across the U.S., primarily in areas of heavy West Indian migration—Washington, D.C., Miami, and New York.

Snapper. This popular Caribbean fish is also a great favorite in the U.S., and is widely available. The meat is white, sweet, and excellent for grilling.

Sorrel, *Hibiscus sabdariffa,* also called roselle, is a tropical flower found throughout the Caribbean. Its bright red sepals are removed from its seed pod and used fresh or dried. It is used to make beverages and jams and can be found packaged dry, year-round, in West Indian markets.

Sweet Potato, *Iomoea batatas,* also called batata and boniato, is a tuberous vegetable native to the Caribbean and Central and South America. The tuber is rich in carbohydrates and it is distinguishable from the North American sweet potato by its oval shape and smooth, reddish skin. It is boiled, baked, grilled, or roasted. It is available in the U.S. in Caribbean markets.

Tamarind, *Tamarindus indica,* is shaped like a pea pod with a brittle, brown skin. The tropical fruit, which has a sour and acid taste, is eaten as a fruit or pulped and used in confectionery, condiments, and beverages. The fresh fruit is sometimes available in Caribbean markets, and the pulp can be found in West Indian and Oriental markets throughout the U.S.

Thyme, *Thymus vulgaris,* is one of the Caribbean's favorite herbs. There are two popular varieties, the broad-leaf French thyme and a smaller, fragrant variety that is more popular. Thyme is usually sold in bundles in the islands and the practice has come to the U.S., where fresh thyme is available in West Indian markets. Thyme is used in soups and stews, as a seasoning rub for roasts, and in fish and poultry dishes.

Yams, *Dioscorea* **sp.,** also called *ñame,* are natives of tropical America. The scores of varieties, including yellow yam, negro yam, and white yam, are cooked like potatoes—peeled and boiled, grilled, baked, or roasted. They are not to be confused with the Louisiana yam. Yams are available in Caribbean markets throughout the U.S.

Yard-Long Beans, *Vigna sesquipedalis,* are also called Chinese beans and boonchi in the Dutch Antilles. The beans, close in taste to green beans, actually grow in lengths of up to 4 feet and are tailormade for the skewer since they wrap around nicely. They are available in Oriental markets throughout the U.S.

Directory of Caribbean Food Distributors

I am happy to report that since doing my last Caribbean Food Directory for *Island Cooking: Recipes from the Caribbean* (The Crossing Press: Freedom, CA) in 1988, island foods have begun to show up on supermarket shelves around the country. The larger cities like New York and Miami are completely saturated with Caribbean markets. Most of the listings, therefore, either pinpoint locations outside of urban centers or list markets that comprise clusters of distributors dealing in Caribbean foods. In New York City, for example, La Marqueta, the Bronx Terminal Market, Hunts Point, and the Brooklyn Terminal Market supply most any Caribbean food product—through hundreds of wholesalers and distributors.

California

Caribbean Delites
1057 E. Artesia Blvd.
Long Beach, CA 90805
(213) 422-5594

Freida's Finest
1950 E. 20th St.
Los Angeles, CA 90058
(213) 627-2981

Jamaica Imports, Ltd.
P.O. Box 90907
Long Beach, CA 90809
(213) 595-9857

La Preferida, Inc.
4615 Alameda St.
Los Angeles, CA 90056
(213) 232-4332
Contact: Ivan Bayona

Stone Bakery and Grocery Co.
6700 S. Crenshaw Blvd.
Los Angeles, CA 90043
(213) 753-3847

A&W Island Foods
2634 San Pablo Ave.
Berkeley, CA 94702
(415) 649-9195

Lee's Enterprises, Ltd.
3910 West Valley Blvd., Unit E
Walnut City, CA 91789
(714) 598-7706
Contact: David Lee

Rosado's International Foods, Inc.
1711 Little Orchard, Ste. B
San Jose, CA 95125
(408) 298-2326

Florida

Blue Mountain Imports, Inc.
7225 N.W. 12th St.
Miami, FL 33126

De Jamaican Shop
4200 N.W. 12th St.
Lauderhill, FL 33313
(305) 581-3990

Royal Distributors
1361 Bennett Dr.
Longwood, FL 32750
(407) 332-0008

Goya
1900 N.W. 92nd Ave.
Miami, FL 33172
(305) 592-3150

Jamaica Groceries & Spices
Colonial Shopping Centre
9628 S.W. 160th St.
Miami, FL 33157
(305) 252-1197

Kingston-Miami Trading Co.
280 N.E. 2nd St.
Miami, FL 33132
(305) 372-9547
or
1500 N.W. 22nd St.
Miami, FL 33142
(305) 324-0231

Ocho-Rios Miami Trading Co.
2051 N.W. 15th Ave.
Miami, FL 33142
(305) 326-1734

Krevatas Import-Export
P.O. Box 562019
Miami, FL 33156
(305) 253-8108

La Preferida, Inc.
9108 N.W. 105th Way
Medley, FL 33178
(305) 883-8444
Contact: Carlos Bordon

McDonald Import Co., Inc.
300 North Chrome Ave.
Florida City, FL 33034
or
P.O. Box 970134
Miami, FL 33197
(305) 246-1816

West Indian American Grocery
19571 N.W. 2nd Ave.
Miami, FL 33169
(305) 651-8455

West Indian Food Specialties
6035 Miramar Pkwy.
Miramar, FL 33023
(305) 962-6418

Chands West Indian &
    Spanish Grocery
2623 North Pine Hills Rd.
Orlando, FL 32808

Georgia

Gourmet Concepts
    International
East Northeast
    Industrial Complex
3519 Church St.
Clarkston, GA 30021
(404) 296-6100

DeKalb's World Farmers
    Market
3000 E. Ponce De Leon
Decatur, GA 30034
(404) 377-6401

Illinois

Goya
2701 West Armitage Ave.
Chicago, IL 60647

La Preferida, Inc.
3400 W. 35th St.
Chicago, IL 60632
(312) 254-7200
Contact: William L. Steinberth
or Robert Gouwens

Island Foods Distributors
705 W. Howard St.
Evanston, IL 60202
(708) 475-1626

Wu Chu Trading Co.
92 S. Water Market St.
Chicago, IL 60602
(312) 633-0927

Maryland

Red Apple
7645 New Hampshire Ave.
Langley Park, MD 20783
(301) 434-1810

Caribbean Market
7505 New Hampshire Ave.
Langley Park, MD 20783
(301) 439-5288

New Jersey

Goya Foods
100 Seaview Dr.
Secaucus, NJ 07094
(201) 348-4900

New York

Bronx Terminal Market
Bronx, NY 10039

Hunts Point Market
Bronx, NY 10474
(718) 542-2900

Island Cooking Kitchens, Inc.
191–201 Powell St.
Brownsville Station, NY 11212
1-800-LUV-JERK

La Preferida, Inc.
945 Close Ave.
Bronx, NY 10473
(718) 589-6800
Contact: Izzy Hoppenfeld

Brooklyn Terminal Market
Liberty Ave.
Brooklyn, NY 11207
(718) 444-5700

La Marqueta
Park Ave. & 111–116th Sts.
New York, NY 10029

Port Royal Foods, Inc.
P.O. Box 881
Hicksville, NY 11802
Contact: Irving Zwecker

Pennsylvania

Not Just Coffee
Main at Levering
Manayunk, PA 19127
(215) 482-8582

Assouline & Ting
314 Brown St.
Philadelphia, PA 19123
(215) 627-3000

Texas

La Preferida, Inc.
4000 Telephone Rd.
Houston, TX 77087
(713) 643-7128
Contact: Edgar Martinez

Caribbean International
5840 Enrose Terrace
Dallas, TX 75227
(214) 319-8477

Washington, D.C.

Continental Tropical Products
1273 4th St., N.E.
Washington, D.C. 20002
(202) 547-4089

International Wholesalers
1234 W. Street, N.E.
Washington, D.C. 20018
(202) 529-0074

Canada

West Indian Fine Foods
Terrace Brae Plaza
Markham & Lawrence
Scarborough, Ont. M1G 1P5
(416) 431-9353

Linstead Market
4561 Sheppard Ave.
Scarborough, Ont. M15 1V3
(414) 292-1053

Solas Market
341 Glendower Circuit
Agincourt
Toronto, Ont. M1T 2M5
(416) 291-6567

Toronto Caribbean Corner
57 Kensington Ave.
Toronto, Ont. M5T 2K2
(416) 593-0008

Central West Indies Grocery
252 Queen St. E.
Eastown Plaza
Brampton, Ont. L6V 1C1
(416) 453-8084

Elma's Spice Corner
2594 Shepard Ave. S.
Mississauga, Ont. L5B 3B2
(416) 277-0557

Harvey W. I. Food Store
2545 Hurontario St.
Mississauga, Ont. L5A 2G4
(416) 272-4950

Dattani Wholesalers
Bay #5, 2219 35th Ave. N.E.
Calgary, Alberta T2E 6W3
(403) 250-8980

Bibliography

The Barbecue Cookbook. Birmingham, Alabama: Oxmoor House, 1988.

Barich, David, and Ingalls, Thomas. *Meat on the Grill.* New York: Harper Collins Publishers, 1993.

Barich, David, and Ingalls, Thomas. *Seafood on the Grill.* New York: Harper Collins Publishers, 1993.

Bastyra, Judy. *Caribbean Cooking.* New York: Exeter Books, 1987.

Belize Cookbook Committee. *A Guide to Belizean Cooking.* Belize: Social Development Department and Ministry of Social Services.

Benghiat, Norma. *Traditional Jamaican Cookery.* London: Penguin Books, 1985.

Bennet, Kim and Debbie. *Charcoal and Woodsmoke.* Edmonton: North Publishing, Ltd., 1984.

Bourne, M. J., Lenox, G. W., and Seddon, S. A. *Fruits and Vegetables of the Caribbean.* London: Macmillan Publishers, Ltd., 1988.

Butel, Jane. *Finger Lickin', Rib Stickin', Great Tastin', Hot and Spicy Barbecue.* New York: Workman Publishing Co., 1982.

Chance, J. L. D. *Ma Chance's French Caribbean Creole Cooking.* New York: Exeter Books, 1987.

Cleary, T. E. *Jamaican Run-Dung.* Kingston, Jamaica: Brainbuster Publications, 1970.

The Cooking of the Caribbean Islands. Foods of the World. New York: Time-Life Books, 1972.

Cook's, July/August 1989.

Dard, Patrice. *Barbecue Cooking, the Gourmet Way.* Les Editions de L'Homme, 1986.

De Mers, John. *Caribbean Cooking.* Los Angeles: HP Books, 1989.

DeWitt, Dave, and Gerlach, Nancy. *The Whole Chile Pepper Book.* Boston: Little, Brown and Company, 1990.

Eat Better, Live Better. New York: The Readers' Digest Association, Inc., 1982.

Eckhardt, Linda. *Barbecue Indoors & Out.* Los Angeles: Jeremy P. Tarcher, Inc., 1986.

Ewald, Ellen. *Recipes for a Small Planet.* New York: Ballantine Books, 1980.

Fenzi, Jewell. *This Is the Way We Cook!* Curaçao, Netherlands Antilles: Thayer-Sargent Publications, 1971.

Gardnier, Kenneth. *Creole Caribbean Cooking.* London: Collins, 1986.

Gerlach, Nancy. "Spicy Salads." *The Whole Chile Pepper,* Spring 1989, pp. 35–44.

The Goya Caribbean Cook's Book. Goya Foods, Inc., 1988.

Greene, Janet, Ruth Herstzberg, and B. Vaughan. *Putting Food By.* New York: Penguin Books, 1988.

Harris, Dunstan. "Caribbean Cooking." *The World and I,* May 1989, pp. 272–77.

Harris, Dunstan. *Island Cooking.* Freedom, CA: The Crossing Press, 1988.

Hingston, Charlotte. *Jill Walker's Cooking in Barbados.* St. Thomas, Barbados: Best of Barbados, Ltd., 1983.

Hudgins, Tom. "Hot Sauces: Fiery Flavorings." 1992 Oxford Symposium on Food and Cookery.

Hughes, Stella. *Chuckwagon Cooking.* Phoenix: The University of Arizona Press, 1974.

Hunt, Sylvia. *Sylvia Hunt's Cooking.* Port of Spain, Trinidad: Scrip-J Printers, Ltd., 1985.

Hurston, Zora Neale. *Tell My Horse: Voodoo and Life in Haiti and Jamaica.* New York: Harper and Row, 1990.

"The Jalapeño." *The Whole Chile Pepper*, Winter 1989, pp. 44–45.

Lewis, M. G. *Journal of a West Indian Proprietor.* London: 1834.

Livingston, A. D. *Grilling, Smoking and Barbecuing.* New York: Lyons and Burford, 1992.

Magic and Medicine of Plants. New York: The Readers' Digest Association, Inc., 1986.

McCune, Kelly. *Vegetables on the Grill.* New York: Harper Collins, 1992.

Morgan, Jinx and Jefferson. "Winning the Barbecue Way." *Bon Appétit,* July 1991, p. 32.

Ortiz, Elizabeth. *The Complete Book of Caribbean Cooking.* New York: M. Evans and Company, 1973.

Ortiz, Elizabeth. *The Complete Book of Mexican Cooking.* New York: Bantam Books, 1965.

Rinzler, Carol Ann. *Herbs, Spices and Condiments.* New York: Facts on File, 1990.

Ritchie, Carson. *Food in Civilization.* New York: Beaufort Books, Inc., 1981.

Robertson, Diane. *Jamaican Herbs.* Kingston, Jamaica: Jamaican Herbs, Ltd., 1982.

Rombauer, I. S., and Becker, M. R. *Joy of Cooking.* New York: Bobbs-Merrill Co., Inc., 1975.

Root, Waverly, and de Rochemont, Richard. *Eating in America—A History.* New York: William Morrow and Co., 1976.

Schlesinger, C., and Willoughby, J. *The Thrill of the Grill.* New York: William Morrow and Co., 1990.

Sinnes, A. C. *The Grilling Encyclopedia.* New York: The Atlantic Monthly Press, 1992.

Slater, Mary. *Caribbean Cooking.* Twickenham, England: Hamlyn Publishing, 1984.

Solomon, Jay. *A Taste of the Tropics.* Freedom, CA: The Crossing Press, 1991.

Springer, R. G. *Caribbean Cookbook.* London: Pan Books, 1979.

Tannahill, Reay. *Food in History.* New York: Crown Publishers, 1989.

Tarantino, Jim. *Marinades.* Freedom, CA: The Crossing Press, 1991.

Trinidad and Tobago Cookbook, ed. Rhona Baptiste. Port of Spain, Trinidad: Imprint Caribbean, Ltd., 1987.

Trinidad and Tobago, Insight Guides. Singapore: APA Publications, 1988.

Voltz, Jeanne. *Barbecued Ribs and Other Great Feeds.* New York: Alfred A. Knopf, 1987.

Waldron, Maggie. *Barbecue and Smoke Cookery.* San Francisco: 101 Productions, 1978.

Whelan, Jack. *Smoking Salmon and Trout.* Vancouver Island: Aerie Publishing, 1982.

The Whole Chile Pepper Catalog, Out West Publishing, 1987.

Willoughby, John, and McCrombie, T. J. "Great Smoked Food." *Cook's,* June 1990, pp. 45–51.

Table of Equivalents

The exact equivalents in the following tables have been rounded for convenience.

US/UK

oz=ounce
lb=pound
in=inch
ft=foot
tbl=tablespoon
fl oz=fluid ounce
qt=quart

Metric

g=gram
kg=kilogram
mm=millimeter
cm=centimeter
ml=milliliter
l=liter

Weights

US/UK	Metric
1 oz	30 g
2 oz	60 g
3 oz	90 g
4 oz ($1/4$ lb)	125 g
5 oz ($1/3$ lb)	155 g
6 oz	185 g
7 oz	220 g
8 oz ($1/4$ lb)	250 g
10 oz	315 g
12 oz ($3/4$ lb)	375 g
14 oz	440 g
16 oz (1 lb)	500 g
$1^{1/2}$ lb	750 g
2 lb	1 kg
3 lb	1.5 kg

Oven Temperatures

Fahrenheit	Celsius	Gas
250	120	$1/2$
275	140	1
300	150	2
325	160	3
350	180	4
375	190	5
400	200	6
425	220	7
450	230	8
475	240	9
500	260	10

Liquids

US	Metric	UK
2 tbl	30 ml	1 fl oz
$1/4$ cup	60 ml	2 fl oz
$1/3$ cup	80 ml	3 fl oz
$1/2$ cup	125 ml	4 fl oz
$2/3$ cup	160 ml	5 fl oz
$3/4$ cup	180 ml	6 fl oz
1 cup	250 ml	8 fl oz
$1^{1/2}$ cups	375 ml	12 fl oz
2 cups	500 ml	16 fl oz
4 cups/1 qt	1 litre	32 fl oz

Length Measures

$1/8$ in	3 mm
$1/4$ in	6 mm
$1/2$ in	12 mm
1 in	2.5 cm
2 in	5 cm
3 in	7.5 cm
4 in	10 cm
5 in	13 cm
6 in	15 cm
7 in	18 cm
8 in	20 cm
9 in	23 cm
10 in	25 cm
11 in	28 cm
12/1 ft	30 cm

Index